PEER TUTORING:
A training and facilitation guide

PEER TUTORING:
A training and facilitation guide

Jesse Pirini

NZCER PRESS

NZCER PRESS
New Zealand Council for Educational Research
PO Box 3237
Wellington
New Zealand
www.nzcer.org.nz

© Jesse Pirini 2017

ISBN 978-0-947509-48-4

No part of the publication may be copied, stored or communicated in any form by any means (paper or digital), including recording or storing in an electronic retrieval system, without the written permission of the publisher.
Education institutions that hold a current licence with Copyright Licensing New Zealand may copy from this book in strict accordance with the terms of the CLNZ Licence.
A catalogue record for this book is available from the National Library of New Zealand

Designed by Smartwork Creative Ltd
Cover design by miss mccabe

This book is for Kate and LP

Contents

Chapter 1 Introduction	1
The key components of effective tutoring	3
How is this book organised?	5
Chapter 2 The tutoring relationship	7
How do you establish a strong tutoring relationship?	9
Mindsets and grit	18
Chapter 3 Tutoring tools and techniques	30
Elements of a tutoring session	30
The tutoring toolbox: How to work with course content	36
A comprehensive model of tutoring	44
Chapter 4 Case studies	46
Traditional school peer tutoring	46
Community homework centre	52
Iwi-based tutoring programme	54
Case studies: Concluding thoughts	57
Chapter 5 Delving into the literature	59
Emotional safety: Why relating well matters	59
Student agency: The importance of giving (and taking) control	61
Goal setting: Why there is no best way	64
Beyond test performance: Metacognitive competencies	67
Chapter 6 Conclusions	72
Appendix 1 Courses, Goals, and Roles Sheet	75
Appendix 2 Goals and Roles conversation script	76
Appendix 3 Grit Scale	78
Appendix 4 Session tracker	82
Appendix 5 Student issue scenarios	85
References	88
Index	92

Chapter 1 Introduction

In early June 2014 Sean Buck, a 17-year-old secondary school student from Auckland, sat at the dining-room table in his family home. The afternoon sun lit up the table top, reflecting off his school report. Opposite Sean sat his mother, Florence. She drummed her fingers on the table as she looked over at her son.

Sean was in a similar situation to many students in New Zealand. He had just received Not Achieved grades for his NCEA[1] English and was scraping through with Achieved grades for his other classes. As far as Florence could tell, Sean was a good student: he went to all his classes and he seemed to do a bit of work every now and then. He would get a bit frantic and stressed out when assessments were due, but Florence remembered being like that when she was at school.

Florence watched Sean, who stared down at the table. His shoulders were slumped and he wouldn't meet her gaze. She thumbed through Sean's report, looking over the credits he had gained. She was worried about how these low grades would affect Sean's future and couldn't stand seeing him feel like he wasn't smart.

Florence decided she had to do something about the situation. She contacted a local tutoring company and organised a one-to-one tutor for Sean. At the time Cameron was a 4th-year university student studying English literature and anthropology. He had been tutoring in students' homes for the previous 2 years to support himself through university and to develop his interpersonal and teaching skills. Cameron had always been very good at English and, more importantly, he connected well with students.

---

1 National Certificate of Educational Achievement.

After only 10 weeks of tutoring with Cameron, Sean was second in his class for English. Sean's improvement was phenomenal and showed that through tutoring he was able to develop successful strategies to succeed in NCEA English.

The story of Sean's situation is a real one. The purpose of this book is to make the one-to-one tutoring strategies that Cameron used available to anyone running a peer tutoring programme. Although Cameron was a university student, these techniques can also be applied by senior school students and mature junior students.

Not all students experience such great increases in grades from tutoring, but tutoring, done well, can make a major difference to a student's time at school, especially when incorporated as an integral part of a school's academic support system. Students like Sean can make huge gains in their grades. They can also become more confident with their school work and interact more in class.

In fact, many students start to ask more questions in class once they begin tutoring. One student said to me that when she was confused by a topic she used to stop listening. However, after she started working with a tutor she tried to learn as much as she could during class because she knew her tutor could help her fill in any gaps later.

Paying more attention in class is one of the unexpected outcomes of tutoring. In fact, the results from tutoring go far beyond increases in grades, and can permeate many aspects of a student's life. This is not surprising. When we take a holistic view of education and consider the whole student rather than focusing solely on grades, it becomes clear that school is a huge part of a student's life. In order to be effective in the long term a tutor needs to tap into their student's motivations and unique life situation.

Recent research into tutoring outcomes[2] shows that students learn extremely well from tutoring—definitely better than they do alone, and at times better than they do from being in a classroom. However, tutoring is not about replacing classrooms. Many schools run peer tutoring programmes and find these an invaluable part of their academic support system.

What did Cameron do in his 10 weeks with Sean? Why was

---

2 See Chapter 5 for a discussion of the research literature in this area.

Cameron able to help Sean when his parents and his teachers had been unable to? Tutoring is an art form, as is teaching. Although educators can easily find research on approaches to teaching, there is a lack of in-depth information on good-quality tutoring. This book goes some way towards filling that gap.

The key components of effective tutoring

This book focuses on two key components of effective tutoring: *the tutoring relationship* and *tutoring tools*.

The tutoring relationship

Cameron was able to build a strong tutoring relationship with Sean, and that is a key part of successful tutoring. Peer tutors have a great relationship-building advantage. They are close in age to the students they are tutoring and they have recently completed the same courses their students are seeking help with. This similarity in age and experience partly explains why Cameron was so effective.

What is it about relating well to someone that is beneficial for learning? There is strong evidence to suggest that when a student feels comfortable and safe, they are able to think more clearly and explore different approaches without fear of failure. You have probably experienced trying to demonstrate a newly mastered trick or skill for someone and finding you can't do it anymore. This is an example of how stress and learning intersect. Some stress can be useful for peak performance, but when learning new things, people need safety to explore without losing face or feeling shame. A strong tutoring relationship provides this safety.

In addition to the benefits of emotional security, a tutoring relationship produces a sense of reciprocity. Students seek to do well, in part, because they want to live up to the expectations of their tutor. There is ample evidence highlighting the importance of expectations on educational achievement (see Chapter 5). However, there is another reciprocity I want to highlight in tutoring: the sense of obligation to a tutor that can influence a student to put in extra effort. While I don't wish to promote students relying on external sources of motivation, this reciprocity is inherent in any relationship, and tutoring is no different. Building a strong tutoring relationship allows tutors to harness the power of reciprocity.

Another important aspect of the tutoring relationship relates to ways to approach success and failure. Psychologist Carol Dweck has popularised a concept called the "growth mindset" (Dweck, 2006), which refers to the way a student responds to things such as test results. Students with a growth mindset treat both successful and unsuccessful outcomes as feedback on their efforts. As a result, the world becomes a place full of possibilities that can be explored by putting in the right kind of effort, in the right kind of way. The contrasting mindset is a "fixed mindset", where students attribute outcomes to their fixed, pre-determined talents. Over time, no matter how talented someone feels they are, obstacles arise that go beyond a person's natural talents and require considerable effort to overcome. A fixed mindset makes obstacles appear impassable, since students with a fixed mindset see their talent as fixed.

It is clear that psychological concepts such as mindset can play an important role in understanding student success. Tutors can help model a growth mindset and provide feedback that facilitates students to develop this kind of mindset. For example, by praising effort rather than talent, tutors help students to focus on what they *did* to reach an outcome.

A psychological concept related to a growth mindset is *grit*, which refers to perseverance and passion for long-term goals. Students who can continue to pursue a long-term goal that excites them will have much more success reaching goals than those who get distracted or regularly shift their focus.

Tutoring techniques: Elements of a session and the tutoring toolbox

Throughout his work with Sean, Cameron did many things that helped Sean develop his understanding of the course content for English and what it meant to do well at NCEA English. In order to help Sean improve in these areas, Cameron used a range of *tutoring techniques* or *tools*.

Tutoring techniques can be divided into two categories. The first are the overall elements that make up a tutoring session. These are the larger structural units of a tutoring session, and they allow the tutoring session to run smoothly. The elements of a tutoring session are like the plumbing and electrics in a house: they are important to how the house operates, but the occupant of the house is not usually aware they are there. Elements of a tutoring session can be put together in whatever way works for a particular tutor. They include activities such as building a mini agenda for the session, reflecting on prior learning, and reviewing work from the previous week.

The second category of tutoring techniques is the tutoring toolbox. The tutoring toolbox includes activities designed specifically to help students master course content. Emma Blackett (a highly experienced tutor and tutor trainer) worked with me to utilise the findings from the academic literature to develop tutoring tools that can be easily applied in a tutoring session. The tutoring toolbox includes tools such as determining an initial course of action, identifying a specific problem and asking deep, exploratory questions.

These tools can be used to carry out two important tutoring tasks: identifying the often complex issues a student has with mastering course content, and helping students develop mastery of particular aspects of course content. It is important to point out that taking a holistic approach means the tutoring tools are applied within the elements of a tutoring session, which supports the student to challenge themselves, focus on effort, and reflect on their progress. Emma and I continue to train tutors to use these tools, and they have found them very useful.

How is this book organised?

This book is organised to help anyone running, or preparing to run, a peer tutoring programme. The first two chapters address effective tutoring. They focus on the tutoring relationship and specific tutoring techniques. There is some overlap here because tutoring techniques are always underpinned by a strong tutoring relationship. In fact, delivering tutoring techniques well reinforces a strong tutoring relationship. I have already introduced these components, but in Chapters 2 and 3 I expand greatly on this discussion, covering facilitation guides and tutor resources. The tutoring relationship and tutoring techniques are tightly interlinked, but they can be usefully separated out for the purposes of tutor training.

In Chapter 4 I present case studies from peer tutoring programmes in New Zealand. These case studies provide examples of how schools, a community group and an iwi group address the various challenges they face in their particular contexts, and I provide some suggestions for how these programmes might apply the learnings from this book.

The final chapter dives into the literature and makes links between the more practical aspects of Chapters 2 to 4 so that you can explore the areas that interest you most. Tutoring has not received nearly as much academic attention as classroom learning, but much of the research into learning and education can be applied to tutoring. The tools, techniques, and approaches from Chapters 2 and 3 are informed by this literature, and I draw explicit links in Chapter 5. If you are interested in taking some of the ideas in this book further, this chapter will help you get started in the literature.

Finally, the appendices contain a range of useful tools for tutors. These tools are discussed throughout Chapters 2 and 3. They are under a creative commons licence and are freely available to use, with attribution to the author.

Over the past 5 years I have trained hundreds of tutors to deliver thousands of hours of tutoring. I have also conducted a 3-year research project into the interactive aspects of tutoring. This book is a practical guide built on experience with strong links to the academic literature, ranging from classical pedagogical theories such as scaffolding, to findings from neuroscience and business and academic coaching. Whether you are interested in developing a great tutoring programme, improving a current tutoring programme or just being a great tutor, you will find this book useful.

Chapter 2 The tutoring relationship

In this chapter I discuss the importance of the tutoring relationship and offer activities for training tutors to develop and maintain a strong tutoring relationship.

Neuroscientific research supports prioritising the tutoring relationship. Pekrun et al. (2002) suggest that higher-level thinking relies on basic emotional needs having already been met. Students need to feel safe and comfortable in order to learn effectively, and certain brain chemicals are released when students feel emotionally secure. These hormones promote learning. If students don't feel safe and comfortable, their brain releases stress hormones that inhibit higher-level reasoning and logical brain functions.

A strong tutoring relationship underpins successful tutoring. When students relate well to their tutor they feel relaxed and comfortable, and as a result can engage in higher-level thinking. In his workshops Nathan Mikaere-Wallis, an education researcher and facilitator, likens the brain to a garden. Stress produces cortisol, which is like spreading weedkiller all over your freshly planted garden. Emotional safety produces endorphins, which is like spreading fertiliser throughout your garden (in appropriate amounts, of course).

As well as emotional security, a strong tutoring relationship forms a sense of reciprocity and obligation. As I pointed out in Chapter 1, the focus here is *not* on developing reliance on a tutor or enforcing an external motivation. Rather, the emphasis is on making the most of the reciprocity that is present in all strong relationships. Educationist Linda Lambert defines a concept of shared leadership that applies rather nicely to this notion of reciprocity. Lambert claims that leadership becomes

> manifest within the relationships in a community, manifest in the spaces, the fields among the participants, rather than in a set of behaviours performed by an individual leader. (Lambert, 2002, p. 42)

Reciprocity and a sense of respect and obligation manifest themselves in the relationship between the tutor and the student. This reciprocity permeates the life of a student in such a way that when they are in class, preparing to do their homework or studying for a test, they are aware on some level of the relationship with their tutor. This awareness helps students to draw on the tutor as a role model, and to raise their standard of work to meet the expectations established within tutoring.

The concept of reciprocity is inherent in tutoring, mentoring, coaching, and family and community relationships. The Māori concept of tuakana–teina captures the sense of the relationship that I suggest works well for tutoring. A tuakana is a more senior and experienced person, and a teina is a more junior and less experienced person.[1] The terms derive from the reciprocal relationships and role distribution in Māori society between older and younger siblings, and the concept has been adopted as a pedagogical framework by many institutions. As with mentoring or supervision, tuakana–teina focuses on roles such as:

- welcoming the learner
- developing an early personal rapport
- helping the less experienced person to feel successful about their learning
- treating the less experienced person fairly, in an open and honest manner
- giving feedback
- making learning fun.

(MacFarlane, Glynn, Cavanagh, & Bateman, 2007)

It is quite clear that these sorts of tasks fit very closely with relationships such as tutoring, mentoring and supervision. However, Winitana (2012) highlights a subtle difference between traditional approaches

---

[1] See Winitana, 2012, for a more in-depth definition of tuakana–teina.

to tutoring, mentoring and supervision and a tuakana–teina relationship. Winitana points out that tuakana–teina emphasises upholding the mana[2] of all the people involved, and in business and academic settings I would suggest that this includes the institution. In the case of peer tutoring, the school is the overarching institution within which tutors and students operate. We can see, therefore, in the notion of tuakana–teina a wider positioning of the tutor and student relationship within institutions, communities, and family. There can be a lot of power in referencing these relationships during tutoring—for both the tutor and the student. It is up to you how you decide to incorporate these higher-level aspects of the tutoring relationship into your tutoring programme or approach.

In these introductory discussions of the tutoring relationship I have strayed some distance from the concrete moments of tutoring. However, by positioning the tutoring relationship as one that is reciprocal—involving obligations between the tutor and the student, and also to family, community and institutions—I am seeking to emphasise that tutoring is not procedural and focused on a single output (e.g. higher grades). Rather, tutoring is a complex process of relating: between the student and the tutor and in the wider context within which tutoring occurs. Taking this perspective highlights the holistic nature of education and the holistic nature of what it means to be a person embedded within a society. Through my experience I have seen that this sort of understanding of tutoring helps tutors to tackle the really tricky aspects of building and maintaining an effective tutoring relationship.

How do you establish a strong tutoring relationship?

Moving on now to the more concrete moments of tutoring, I consider how the tutor can work to establish a strong tutoring relationship. For some new tutors the idea of a productive tutoring relationship may seem to have less substance than practical tutoring approaches, such as helping a student to write a paragraph, solve an equation, or prepare a report. But a productive tutoring relationship is actually built upon

---

2 Here I define mana as *prestige* and *character*. However, see Tomlins-Jahnke & Mulholland (2011) for an in-depth discussion of the concept of mana, because it is difficult to provide a single-word definition of the concept.

concrete actions taken by the tutor. These include things such as the way the tutor speaks to the student and the types of activities the tutor introduces. In this section I outline some practical ways a tutor can develop a tutoring relationship with a student, and also how tutors can be trained to build a tutoring relationship.

I have found there are two concrete actions that tutors can use to establish a productive tutoring relationship: *goal and roles conversation* and *building and maintaining a sense of agreement*. The goals and roles conversation lays the groundwork for a strong tutoring relationship, and the sense of agreement refers to techniques for maintaining a strong tutoring relationship. This section will help people running, or setting up, tutoring programmes to think carefully about how to structure their programme to support productive tutoring relationships.

Building a tutoring relationship: Part 1—Goals and roles conversation

The very first thing I always do with students is have a discussion about what courses or subjects they are taking and why they are getting tutoring. I also discuss how tutoring sessions can work, and explore the student's expectations. In order to carry out this conversation I use a "Courses, Goals and Roles Sheet", which you can find in Appendix 1. It is important to ask students to list all of the courses/subjects they are taking because this can help tutors understand what sort of student they are working with.

For example, some students take lots of maths- and science-related subjects, some take more writing- and language-based subjects, and some take a combination. The mix of subjects a student is taking might give the tutor some insight into what subjects a student likes, where their strengths may lie and what future study options they have available. While a tutor's speciality might be English, taking a holistic approach to tutoring means knowing all the subjects a student is taking. At the very least this means that a tutor recognises the student has other subjects they need to focus on beyond English. This becomes important as students start to have multiple assessments and assignments due and need to manage their time carefully.

Once a tutor knows what courses/subjects a student is taking, they can start to ask their student why he or she is getting tutoring. On the

"Courses, Goals and Roles Sheet" is a space that allows the student to fill out three goals for the year. Although the sheet refers to goals, the most important part of this process is not the goals themselves but the type of conversation that talking about goals facilitates.

Goals help the tutor to develop an understanding of their student. This includes understanding how the student likes to think about goals, and also what they want to get out of tutoring. What is important to them? Tapping into what drives a student will help a tutor get the best results. For the student, goals provide a context and a purpose for the tutoring session. Because they are set and worked on *by the student*, goals help students develop the traits of independent learners.

Tutors must understand that people set goals in many different ways. Some people set goals for every part of their lives, write these down and then carefully track their progress. I was running a tutor training once and a tutor arrived with specific goals written down detailing what they wanted to get out of the training. This highly goal-oriented approach will put some people off. They prefer to take things as they come. They don't like talking about a specific goal, and setting goals in a specific way does not motivate or support them.

A moment from a tutor training highlights the importance of recognising the different approaches people take to goal setting. At a training in 2013 I was role-playing a goals conversation with about 10 tutors. A tutor called Sandy was playing the role of the tutor, and another tutor, Harry, was playing the role of the student. Sandy and Harry had set one goal for the year, and Sandy was asking Harry if he had any other goals he wanted to achieve. Sandy kept trying to draw Harry into setting more goals. Eventually Harry got very angry and defensive and swore at Sandy. Even though this was a role-play, the idea of setting goals brought up some past feelings for Harry that were uncomfortable. Sandy had not picked up on this, and for her, setting lots of specific goals was a good thing. Sandy had been insensitive to Harry's agitation and to the possibility that there are different ways of setting goals or thinking about the future.

While it is important to be aware of individual differences regarding goals, a conversation about goals is absolutely crucial to the tutoring relationship. A goals conversation must be carried out artfully and for the right reasons. Helping tutors understand *why* they are having a goals conversation means they can work with students who approach goals in a different way to them.

Remember, there is not one best way to set goals. Writing goals down, setting SMART (Specific, Measureable, Achievable, Realistic, Time-bound) goals and tracking performance are not necessarily the right things to do for everyone during tutoring. For example, there has been some criticism of goals from the business community because they can lack emotional engagement and are often procedural. In the case of performance reviews, for example, goals can become a mere 'tick box' activity.

School students are also sometimes prompted to set goals for the year in class. I once worked with a student who dejectedly pulled out a list of three uninspiring goals when I asked her what she wanted to get out of our tutoring. She had set these goals in class and thought that we were about to do the same sort of activity to begin our tutoring. I had to assure her that our *goals conversation* was much more about getting to know one another and helping me learn what she wanted out of tutoring rather than arbitrarily coming up with a list of three goals.

The purpose of discussing goals in a tutoring session is to:

- understand what kind of student the tutor is working with
- develop some vision of a new futurebuild a platform to talk about roles and expectations.

With this in mind, tutors can carry out an effective goals conversation as a way to get to know their student, and then progress to talk about roles and expectations.

How to carry out an effective goals and roles discussion

I have developed a guide to carrying out an effective goals and roles conversation. Tutors can use this guide to help them get a fuller picture of what a student wants out of tutoring.

Often students take some time to warm up, and their first response to a goals-related question might be quite shallow. Students might say something like "Well, I just want to pass", and then look at the tutor like they are an idiot for asking such a foolish question. The questions in the goals and roles conversation will help the tutor explore the student's motivation more deeply than these surface-level responses.

Some students find exams stressful, and so focusing on relaxed exam performance will be a useful focus for them. Some students might be targeting a certain university course, which in turn contributes to a focus for tutoring. The goals aspect of the conversation helps tutors explore the student's experience of school. Building on the goals discussion, the roles and expectations aspect helps the student realise the tutor is there to help them with whatever they need help with. In turn, this approach develops a sense of agency for the student.

Facilitation ideas

Using a line-up to demonstrate variation in goal setting behaviour

Target outcome: Tutors understand that everyone sets goals differently.
Activity: The facilitator indicates that one side of the room represents a '10' on a scale of goal setting. A 10 represents someone who sets goals for everything. This type of person writes their goals down and carefully tracks their progress. The facilitator then sets up the other side of the room to represent a '1'. A 1 is a person who never sets goals, who prefers to go with the flow, who doesn't track anything, and who is probably a little put off by the idea of goals. Then the tutors are invited to arrange themselves along this imaginary scale where they feel their goal-setting behaviour fits.
Discuss: Choose a person from each end and someone in the middle and ask them to discuss why they put themselves there. You will generally find a large spread of people.

All the tutors I have worked with are very high-achieving students, so it is not true to say there is a certain type of goal-setting behaviour that is most effective. This activity highlights that fact. Before I started doing this activity I used to just ask tutors how they set goals. Often those who really enjoyed setting goals would take the opportunity to preach about the importance of goals, while those who did not like setting goals were left feeling they were doing something wrong. Over time I have come to believe that most people have some sense of the life they want. Their approach to goal setting simply reveals how they frame the world and their place in it. Of course, how a student frames the world is crucial information for a tutor, hence the importance of a goal-setting conversation.

The facilitator can then point out that an '8' tutor might find themselves working with a '2' student, or vice versa, and since there is no *best* way to set goals, the 8 and 2 tutors will need to be flexible in their goals conversation.

Real-play using goals and roles conversation script

Target outcome: Tutors practise running a 'courses and goals' conversation with another person. They experience the challenge of talking about goals with someone. Tutors also experience being asked about their own goals.

Activity: The facilitator gives each tutor a copy of the "Goals and Roles Conversation Sheet" and a "Courses, Goals and Roles Sheet" (see Appendix 1 and Appendix 2, respectively). In pairs, or groups of three, each person takes a turn being a tutor and being a student. Using groups of three the third member can observe what works and what does not when they are not playing the role of tutor or student. Sometimes, being the observer is the most effective learning position as they have space to reflect on the interaction as it occurs.

The term 'real-play' is used to highlight the focus of this activity on trying to run an authentic goals conversation. Tutors are often also students so they can act as if they are getting tutoring for their own subjects, or they can cast their minds back to when they were in high school and pretend they are getting tutoring for a subject they found difficult. At times people resist real-plays, or find them a little awkward. But once they find themselves in a real tutoring situation, the conversation they had during a real-play will be the first thing they draw on as they figure out what to do.

It is important that the facilitator demonstrates the goals conversation in front of the group before the activity. The facilitator should take the real-play as seriously as possible, even announcing what day and time the tutoring is happening (e.g. "It's Thursday afternoon, 4pm, and I've just met this student for the first time"). As a facilitator, ask someone from the group to volunteer to 'be a student' in front of the group and run through a full goals and roles conversation with them. If you have never run such a conversation before, it is worth practising a few times with various people so that a few different situations come up. Even if this conversation does not go that well, it will help students get an idea of what they should be doing.

Goals and roles conversation script
(see also Appendix 2)

There are many different types of goals and ways of bringing up goals. Here's one formula you could try. Or you could pick out certain aspects of this and use them in your own way.

1. Ask a general question about how school is going. Aim to get a narrative about how things are—what is good, what is not so good:
    - What would it look like if it were just a Tiny Bit Better?
    - What would it look like if it were a Little Bit Better?
    - What would it look like if it were a Lot Better?
    - What would it look like if it were Perfect?
2. Gather more details with questions like these:
    - Why do you want to achieve that goal?
    - Where do you think this goal will lead to?
    - What will a goal like this help you do?
    - What is involved in achieving this goal?
3. The essential outcome is to create a real sense of a better future and that the student chooses goals for themselves. At this stage you might be able to ask the student to write down one, two or three key goals.
4. You might like to suggest a mix of process goals (e.g. I will do 3 x 20 minutes of maths homework a week) and outcome goals (e.g. I will get a Merit endorsement).

Roles and expectations

Building on this vision of the future, you can now discuss how tutoring can help the student get there. You might start with the following questions:
1. What do you think I can do to help you reach these goals?
2. What do you think you might need to do to reach these goals, and how can I help you do that?

Lastly, contribute your own ideas about how the tutoring sessions can operate. Ask the student to take a few notes regarding roles and expectations on the Courses, Goals and Roles Sheet.

Moving on...

At this stage, I suggest moving on to finding out how organised the student is and what their capabilities are. Here are some suggestions:
- Ask about what assessments they have for the year, when these are and how they feel about each of them
- Ask about their study habits, time management and organisation of school material (notes, etc.) Do a small test of their ability or knowledge, or ask to see a sample of work.

Building a tutoring relationship: Part 2—Working with a sense of agreement

A well-executed goals discussion develops a *sense of agreement*. A sense of agreement refers to a shared sense of the purpose of tutoring. Obviously if tutors have a good discussion with students early on then each has a clear idea about why they are attending the tutoring. There is an emphasis here on tutors developing their listening skills in order to allow students to fully explore their reasons for tutoring.

In my experience students respond very well to being asked what they want out of tutoring because they realise the tutor is there to help them with their problems. All students have some issues they are a little nervous or worried about regarding school work, and knowing that a tutor will help them with these is motivating. Asking for student input into tutoring contrasts with a traditional classroom approach, where the teacher is in charge and directs the class. A one-to-one tutoring session usually has more opportunities for establishing shared responsibility and providing students with the space to direct their learning.

A sense of agreement can change over time and is a bit like a plant. You must water and feed your sense of agreement for it to thrive. In practice, tutors need to return regularly to the sense of agreement or the shared purpose of tutoring. While the sense of agreement is established through the initial goals conversation, it is maintained by the multiple minor interactions that students and tutors have during tutoring. The tutor is responsible for maintaining the sense of agreement, and this can be as simple as checking in with a student to confirm how they are feeling about the goals they discussed, or making sure the activities they carry out in tutoring are helping the student.

In a synthesis of educational research Adrienne Alton-Lee highlights the importance of enabling students to take charge of their own learning. However, she points out that this does not mean unstructured 'discovery'. Rather, Alton-Lee advocates for an approach that is highly structured in order to support student agency and sustained, thoughtful engagement. In a 2003 report for the Ministry of Education, Alton-Lee stated that sustained higher academic achievement is possible through

> foster[ing] students' abilities to define their own learning goals, ask questions, anticipate the structure of curriculum experiences, use metacognitive strategies when engaging with curriculum, and self-monitor. (Alton-Lee, 2003, p. 93)

Alton-Lee recognises what many other researchers have highlighted for many years: there is power in taking meaningful action and seeing the results of our decisions and choices. Alton-Lee's work encourages teachers to provide students with opportunities to take control of their learning in ways that result in meaningful actions. However, in a classroom setting, with the pressures of assessment looming, teachers can struggle to do more than focus on a surface-level approach focusing on coping with content.

Tutoring, in contrast, can sit outside the mass education system and provide opportunities for student agency. The sense of agreement, established through an authentic goal-setting conversation, targets student engagement by asking them to define their own learning goals through the goals conversations and then continually returning to these, either to update the learning goals or update the approaches taken to achieve them.

Returning to the sense of agreement is an excellent way to hold students accountable. For example, often students will not complete as much work as is required to get the results they want. Tutors can refer to the sense of agreement as a way to highlight the discrepancy between work done and work required. Referring to the previously made agreement means the student is really holding themselves accountable (to themselves). This is a crucial independent learning skill, which tutors can help students develop.

Here is an example of how a conversation addressing a sense of agreement might go.

Example conversation maintaining a sense of agreement

Tutor: Have you finished the questions we set last week?

Student: No, I didn't quite get through them all. I was really busy with rugby training, and then I lost the sheet, and I think my dog was sick for a while.

Tutor: OK, well this is the third time you haven't done the questions, and you need to do the questions to do well in the final exam. When we started tutoring you set a goal of 'Achieved for algebra'. Is that still the case, or has that changed?

In the sample conversation above the tutor draws on the sense of agreement to emphasise the importance of doing the practice questions during the week. You can see that a well-developed goals and roles discussion lays a foundation for the future. Because the tutor helped the student establish a goal—or a vision for the future—that was owned by the student, the tutor can now draw on that goal-setting discussion to hold the student accountable for doing their homework. In this context, the goals and roles discussion becomes extremely important to the ongoing tutoring relationship.

In addition, the tutor is making sure the sense of agreement is maintained. A student may have set a goal that is too hard for them, or they may have lost interest in a goal such as getting Achieved in algebra. It is hard, but a tutor needs to follow what the student wants in these situations. In most cases a conversation like the one above can lead to finding ways to carve out time to do homework questions, or delving deeper into why the student is not doing their homework (e.g. they still don't understand how to do the work, they don't have a good work routine, they do actually lose things, etc.).

However, in some rare cases, especially if students do not participate and if the student is not engaged in tutoring, then tutoring needs to end. I have had to cancel tutoring with students in the past, although this is not common. Cancellation is an important option for tutors, because tutoring only works when the student participates. I believe there is no point continuing with tutoring if the student is not participating. In fact, the option of cancellation shows the student that their learning is up to them, in turn supporting their own agency. I would like to emphasise that cancellation is very rare, and in almost all cases addressing the sense of agreement helps students to re-engage in tutoring, either by reminding them why they are there or by re-directing the tutoring along a more suitable path.

Mindsets and grit

I have outlined the two key ways that tutors can establish and maintain a tutoring relationship. Specifically, they can:

- conduct a goals conversation as soon as possible with the student to establish an overall purpose for tutoring

- maintain their focus on the sense of agreement between themselves and the student and work to maintain the sense of agreement when required.

In Chapter 3, where I examine the elements of a tutoring session and the tutoring toolbox, I will explore further techniques for establishing and maintaining the tutoring relationship.

I would now like to move on to examine another higher-level aspect of tutoring. This aspect is the mindset with which a tutor approaches tutoring and the skills a tutor models. Given that a strong tutoring relationship incorporates an aspect of role-modelling, what are effective learning approaches that a tutor can role-model? Here I explore the related notions of a *growth mindset* and *grit*.

Over the past 30 years, research in psychology has begun to focus on what it is that helps people to be successful. Studies have looked at success in many different domains, including music, science, creative writing, arts, business, the military and sports. One of the major defining features of people achieving great results in these fields has been their ability to persist in the face of challenges, and the way they respond to setbacks. Let me give an example.

At the 2008 Olympics, American swimmer Michael Phelps won eight gold medals. One of these medals came from the 4 x 100 freestyle relay. What is truly remarkable about this win was how unlikely it was. Each relay team is made up of four swimmers, and each swimmer completes a 100-metre freestyle swim, which in an Olympic distance pool is two lengths.

Prior to the race the combined individual 100-metre times of the American relay team was more than 2 seconds slower than those for the French team. The French team also included the world record holder for the 100-metre freestyle, Alain Bernard. Bernard is a bear of a man at 1.93m, and he would be swimming the final leg of the relay. For these reasons this medal was considered one of the least likely for Phelps to win.

Phelps swam the first leg of the relay, so he was left to watch the final three swimmers determine whether he could continue to pursue his goal of eight golds. It was going to be a fast race. The very first Australian swimmer, Eamon Sullivan, broke Alain Bernard's world record for the 100metres freestyle with a 47.05-second swim. In a relay only the first swimmer can set a world record for the 100-metres freestyle, because of the possibility of subsequent swimmers gaining a 'drafting' advantage from swimmers in front of them in adjacent lanes.

Jason Lezac was swimming the final leg of the relay for the Americans. He was the oldest swimmer in the team and was at his third Olympics. By the time Lezac entered the water the Americans were almost a full body length behind the French. Things were not looking good for Phelps and his team. Not only was Lezac racing against Alain Bernard, but he was starting from behind. It looked like what many analysts had predicted: the French were simply too fast for the Americans.

Lezac stayed about three-quarters of a body length behind Bernard for the first 50 metres. At the turn he gained some ground and was about half a body length behind. This was a France/USA race, and no other teams were in the frame for gold at this stage. In fact, it didn't even look as if the Americans were in the frame for gold. On the video the US commentator can be heard saying, "At least they'll be likely to get a silver".

Then the unbelievable started to happen. Lezac began to gain on Bernard. With 25 metres to go the gap was closing. Inexplicably Bernard started to tense up. Over the final 10 metres Lezac somehow surged forward and he was neck and neck with Bernard at the finish. The final time flashed on the boards and showed that Lezac won the race by the smallest margin possible: 0.01 seconds.

It turned out that Lezac swam a 46.06-second race. To put this in context we need to look at the times the members of his team swam:

- Michael Phelps: 47.51
- Garrett Weber-Gale: 47.02
- Cullen Jones: 47.65
- Jason Lezac: 46.06.

Lezac's time stands out as unbelievable in this context. He was a full second faster than the current world record for the 100-metre freestyle, and even though he had a drafting advantage he was still 1 second ahead of other swimmers in his team that had similar drafting advantages swimming the second and third legs of the relay.

How was Lezac so fast over the last leg of this race? The purely physical reason is that Lezac was able to draft off Bernard. Drafting in swimming means positioning yourself as close as possible to the lane rope in order to benefit from the wake produced by the other swimmer. The wake can reduce some of the water friction, and a big wake pulls a swimmer along. You've probably seen images of dolphins playing in the wake of a boat. They are enjoying the speed advantage of the wake. Bernard is a big man and he produces a big wake. Swimming commentators also suggest that Lezac's looping stroke is well suited to drafting.

Many swimmers are able to gain some drafting advantage in relays. In fact, Lezac claims he has had many swimmers draft off him, and so he saw this as his chance to take some of that advantage back. Drafting might help, but no swimmer prefers to be second in a relay so that they can draft. Being in front is always a better place to be.

I want to focus here on Lezac's mindset entering the race and entering the water. The mindset that he brought to the final leg of the relay is what brought together all of his physical training and the potential to draft off Bernard, who for some unknown reason was swimming very close to his lane rope, making drafting more likely. This notion of mindset is so powerful because it provides that extra *something*. I like to call mindset the 'secret sauce' of success. Without mindset you can have everything required to do well and fail to bring it all together effectively to perform. Swimming commentators refer to the 'final leg' mindset that some swimmers have. Some swimmers—Lezac being one of them—are greatly suited to anchoring the final leg of a relay because it fires them up and they swim better in a team environment.

While swimming might seem an unusual metaphor for academic success, really it is very closely related. Swimming takes regular practice and a focus on both physical fitness and technique. For me, I liken this to making sure that students put in the time studying, but also that they continue to refine the *way* they study. Simply spending hours at a desk is not enough: students have to apply themselves deliberately to be successful academically. Lastly, they have to have the mindset to bring everything together, both during ongoing periods of study and when they are required to perform during exams and assessments (race day!).

A lot of education research focuses on what students should do when they study and how much time they should put into studying.

However, the findings from psychological research into motivation and perseverance have revealed that mindset and grit are in fact very strong predictors of success in various fields. But what exactly are mindset and grit, and can they be developed in students? Mindset and grit are not the lengths you put in during swimming training, and they are not the amount of time and effort you put into exam preparation. Mindset and grit are something other than the work students do. Mindset and grit can be usefully thought of as a framework within which the work gets done. Mindset and grit colour the way students approach their study time, their tests and assessments, and their results.

Mindset: Carol Dweck and the growth mindset

A young psychologist, Carol Dweck, was looking over her data from a recent study. She had the exam and test results of hundreds of medical school students laid out in front of her. Carol compared the students' exam and test results with the myriad measures and data she had collected from those same students. Carol had a burning question in her mind: What was it that separated the good students from the bad students? Of course, all the students that had made it as far as medical school were good. But what made some students drop out while others succeeded? What made some students reach the top of the class while others sat in the middle range or below?

In pursuit of insight into these questions Carol had measured many things. She had measured the IQ of each of the students, and she had collected data on their family backgrounds, on their previous test scores and on their health and social activities. Over time it became clear to Carol that what separated the best students from the rest was not some measure of IQ. It was the ways in which students responded to setbacks. Some students failed a test and never returned; others failed and came back to do better and better. Over the past 30 years Carol Dweck[3] has popularised the notion of mindset to describe these differences, in particular, the *growth mindset*.

Students with a growth mindset believe their success and failure are due to their own efforts and actions. Students with the opposite mindset, a fixed mindset, believe they have fixed talents and abilities, which allow them to succeed. When a student with a fixed mindset fails a test,

---

3 See Dweck (2006) for a full exposition of the growth mindset.

they respond by blaming their fixed talent or ability. Because these talents or abilities are fixed, they have a limited range of responses. These responses include things like blaming the test, or blaming their lack of talent. Even students who do very well can operate with a fixed mindset. Challenges in life and education become more and more difficult over time, and regardless of how talented a student is they will eventually reach a level where they find they no longer have enough talent to continue progressing.

In contrast, students with a growth mindset respond to challenges by analysing their preparation and performance, looking for what worked and what did not. This approach gives students something to work on, areas to develop, things to change and things to continue. The idea of a growth mindset tends to paint a rather rosy picture of positive, happy students analysing their performance and continually developing. In practice, applying a growth mindset is a difficult process of self-exploration and (productive) critique. It takes time and effort to continually analyse your performance and preparation. Perhaps as a result of the effort involved, students often approach some areas of their life with a fixed mindset and other areas with a growth mindset. In these cases tutors can be instrumental in helping students to see how they can apply a growth mindset more liberally, or more specifically in the areas they wish to improve in.

As I described above, students with a fixed mindset rely on their talents (or lack of) to explain poor performance. They also shift responsibility for their poor performance to external factors, rather than considering how they can respond to these factors next time.

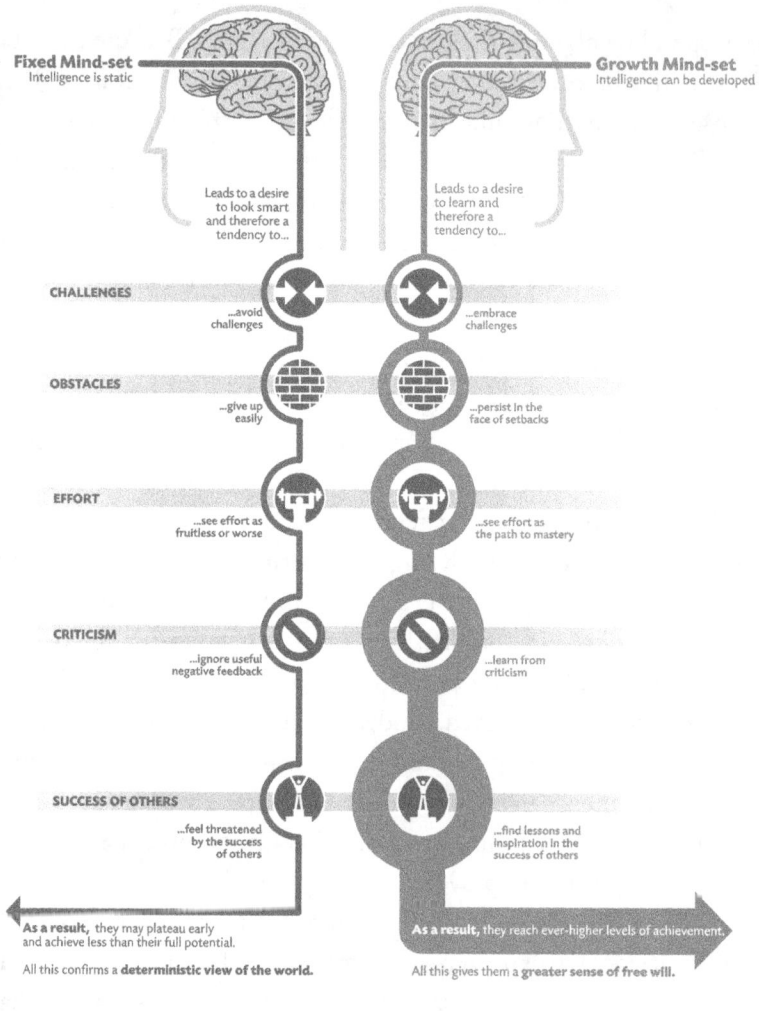

Figure 1: Comparison between Fixed and Growth Mind-sets
(Source: www.nigelholmes.com)

How do you influence students to develop a growth mindset?

Since Carol Dweck started developing the idea of a growth mindset it has been tested in hundreds of different scientific studies. Scientists have demonstrated remarkable differences between students with a growth mindset and students with a fixed mindset across a variety of activities.

More importantly, many researchers have now shown that students develop a growth or fixed mindset over time (Dweck, 2006). They have also shown that very small changes can influence the type of mindset a student brings to an exam or assessment situation. The type of praise a parent, tutor, or teacher gives a student influences whether they develop a growth mindset. In one early study (Mueller & Dweck, 1998) researchers separated students into two groups and directed them to complete a quiz. They then praised each group. They praised the first group with comments such as, "You did great, you must be really smart", and they praised the second group with comments such as, "You did great, you must have worked hard". After that they asked each group what sort of problem they would like to work on next. It turned out that the majority of the children who were praised for their intelligence wanted to do the easy task that was in their comfort zone. The majority of the children praised for the process (i.e. working really hard) wanted to do the more challenging task, which they could learn from.

Later they gave all the children really challenging problems, and they found that the ones who had been praised for being intelligent became discouraged and disengaged, while those who were praised for working hard kept going and remained engaged. Dweck theorises that students praised for being intelligent lose confidence when tasks become difficult, because if success means you are intelligent then failure means you are not.

At its core the growth mindset is about responding to challenges by taking responsibility for your actions and your performance. The way a growth mindset permeates many aspects of students' lives in positive ways is impressive, and therefore a critical role for tutors is to help students to develop or maintain a growth mindset.

In practice, developing a growth mindset in students requires tutors to themselves act with a growth mindset. When tutors possess a growth mindset, all their actions are congruent with this mindset. Each comment they make, the way they approach tutoring sessions and the type of feedback they provide reflects a growth mindset. As we saw with the study above, certain types of comments and questions help students to develop a growth mindset.

The goals discussion and the notion of working with a sense of agreement are built upon a growth mindset approach to learning. One easy way to think of a growth mindset is where one attributes their success. A person with a growth mindset attributes their success to *the work and effort they have put in*. A person with a fixed mindset attributes their success to *their latent, or fixed, talents or abilities*. The goals discussion focuses on the work the student will do in order to realise some better future. A well-structured goals conversation promotes *working with a sense of agreement,* which highlights the work the student needs to do in order to get the most out of their tutoring. We can see how a goals conversation, maintained through regular attention to the sense of agreement, focuses tutoring on the work a student needs to do. By focusing on the work and effort of the student, tutoring promotes a growth mindset.

In Chapter 3, where we delve more deeply into specific tutoring tools, we will see how these tools also promote a growth mindset. One point I would like to make here is this: just telling people they should have a growth mindset is not enough. We need to involve people in interactions with teachers, tutors and course material that promote a growth mindset approach. Many schools are now working with the growth mindset concept, so it is important for tutors to utilise the same concept.

Grit: The benefits of perseverance and passion

Tutors are uniquely positioned to help students see the benefits of regular, consistent work towards a goal. This section will examine the notion of grit, which has emerged as a powerful predictor of successful goal attainment. Defined as perseverance and passion for long-term goals (Duckworth, Peterson, Matthews, & Kelly, 2007), grit overlaps many related concepts such as perseverance, resilience and conscientiousness. Tutors can apply the notion of grit with their students, aiming to increase their perseverance and passion, and help them to understand what it means to be 'gritty'.

Angela Lee Duckworth is a psychologist, but she started off her career as a business consultant. She studied at an Ivy League college in the US, took a scholarship to Cambridge University in the UK, and then joined a large consulting firm to start her working career. At the age of 30 Duckworth returned to academic study in psychology. She characterises her first 10 years of study and work as a pursuit of many different goals.

In a TEDx talk Duckworth (2013) compares herself to a speedboat going first in one direction, then another, and then another. The speedboat might get places quickly but it never gets anywhere in particular.

She argues that while she saw considerable success, she was not on a path to achieving any specific long-term goal.

While many people would be happy with the achievements that Duckworth made, she herself was not happy with what she was doing. She yearned for something more. After beginning studies in psychology towards a PhD, Duckworth came across the notions of perseverance, ambition and conscientiousness. She determined that in her career she had not displayed perseverance and had lacked passion for a specific future. Instead she had hopped from one shiny goal to another.

Whether or not you agree with Duckworth's assessment of her own achievements, she has shown that the concept of grit is a useful predictor of success in a variety of different settings. She developed a Grit Scale and applied it to different groups of people. She found that scoring highly on the Grit Scale predicted:

- a higher grade point average in college students
- retention in a military cadet programme
- better performance in a spelling bee.

Duckworth argues that the Grit Scale is a useful measure of the concept of grit, and that grit, in turn, enables people to persevere in pursuing a goal over an extended period of time, despite obstacles and challenges.

The evidence that Duckworth and colleagues have collected supports these conclusions.[4] At this stage there is little evidence examining how people might develop grit as a personality trait, and there are arguments that personality traits are in fact fixed. However, it seems clear to me that tutors can help students persevere towards a future state and help them explore their passion for various future states.

Grit also emphasises the importance of students having the chance to experience setbacks, face challenges and find ways to get past these. A tutor should not insulate a student from experiencing difficulty, but rather provide support and guidance. This is a challenging balance to strike, but it is possible and requires trust from the tutor that the student will find their own path as long as they are given the opportunity and support to explore.

---

4 This evidence has been contested (Credé, Tynan, & Harms, 2016), and Duckworth has conceded some of these points. I continue to use the concept of grit because it provides a useful way to talk about perseverance and conscientiousness.

Applying grit in tutoring

Duckworth's Grit Scale test can be taken by anyone in about 15 minutes. The scale involves 12 questions, with five possible answers. Each answer is worth a certain number of points, and after a simple calculation reveals a score from 1 to 5. There are, of course, some issues with this kind of self-test. A major one is the transparency of the test as a measure of grit and the social desirability of being perceived as someone who is gritty. People taking this test might therefore seek to answer in a way that produces a high grit score.

In tutoring I prefer to use a concept such as grit to help people explore their personality and think about how they like to approach various tasks. Grit is also related to age, with people becoming more 'gritty' the older they get. Duckworth and colleagues suggest that a desire for novelty and a low threshold for frustration may be good for young people, who will move on from dead-end pursuits and discover more promising paths. However, they point out that excellence takes time, and that "discovery must at some point give way to development" (Duckworth et al., 2007, p. 1092).

Taking the test

Tutors might find it useful to take the grit test themselves and use the test to think about what goals they have that they are passionate about, and how their pursuit of these goals is, or is not, gritty. (See Appendix 3 for the test.)

I personally find it quite empowering to think that the path to a goal requires grit, because grit highlights the fact that achieving goals is difficult and that setbacks are all part of the process. For me, this removes the power of setbacks to discourage pursuit of a goal. Reframing setbacks as a sign that you are on track towards a challenging goal can be a powerful tool.

I encourage tutors to take the grit test in the context of their own lives because it helps them work with students and the concept of grit. It is common for new teachers to be very harsh markers and to set incredibly high standards. I think the same is true for tutors who have not deeply explored their own goals. They can expect students to almost immediately achieve difficult goals and overcome significant learning challenges. In order to overcome the expectation of too-high standards, it is important for tutors to become self-critical and understand their own grit before bringing up grit with students.

In conclusion, when it comes to grit, the concept is useful to continue to delve into the notion of goals and what it means to progress towards goals. A conversation about grit, framed by taking the grit test, can be useful in follow-up sessions after goal conversations. In addition, a grit conversation can be particularly useful after students have had a setback.

Grit can also be used to help students develop a growth mindset by seeing that persistent work is what matters for excellence. The focus on persistent work highlights a student's influence on the world and the growth potential that exists when they persevere in pursuit of a goal.

Chapter 2 Summary: Key points about the tutoring relationship

- Students need to feel safe to learn. This safety comes from a strong relationship with their tutor.
- A strong relationship develops a sense of respect and obligation between the tutor and student. This is a powerful force that helps the student learn.
- The tutoring relationship can be positioned within larger frameworks of family, community and institutions.
- Tutoring relationships are established through the concrete moments where the tutor and student interact.
- Two models can help guide tutors in their relationship building. These are: 1. Goals and Roles Conversation (p. 10), and 2. Building and maintaining a sense of agreement (p. 16).
- A growth mindset (p. 22) and grit (p. 26) are both ways of thinking and acting that are best modelled via a strong tutoring relationship.

Chapter 3 Tutoring tools and techniques

After examining the tutoring relationship, mindset and grit in the previous chapter, I now focus in more detail on how tutors can structure individual tutoring sessions. During tutoring sessions tutors can use a range of approaches to help students structure their thinking and overcome specific challenges. First, I examine the structural building blocks of tutoring sessions. These building blocks are the various *elements* that make up a tutoring session. After that I focus on more specific *tools* that tutors can apply to help students with particular issues. Overall this chapter will describe how tutors can structure their tutoring sessions and address specific student issues with course content knowledge and skills.

Elements of a tutoring session

During a tutoring session tutors provide a structure for students to explore their own learning. When using this approach, tutors focus first on helping the student manage their own learning, and then on subject content as and when required. Adult teaching expert Dean Nugent first introduced me to the metaphor of teaching as the plumbing and electrics in a house. As a facilitator teaching others to teach adults, Dean would 'expose' the plumbing and electrics to us while he taught. It was artfully done, and the importance of providing a framework for students to work within has stuck with me ever since.

The importance of providing a content-free structure that facilitates student learning is illustrated by a group of researchers who advocate *making thinking visible.* I provide a link to their book in Chapter 5, where I introduce links to the academic literature (Ritchhart, Church & Morrison, 2011). Their basic premise is that thinking is doing, and that the notion of a thinker sitting in silence with their chin resting on their fist is only one of many possible ways to think. The making thinking visible group have produced a range of thinking routines that can be used in many situations to help kick start a person's or group's thinking. These thinking routines are content-free and so can be used in many situations.

One example of a thinking routine made visible is called *Think Puzzle Explore* (Ritchart et al., 2011). In this routine students answer three questions:

- What do you think you know about this topic?
- What questions or puzzles do you have?
- How can you explore this topic?

This routine helps students to access prior knowledge, stimulate their curiosity and begin independent inquiry. You can see that a thinking routine like this provides a structure for thinking through problems. Similarly, the elements of tutoring provide a framework for students to explore their ideas, manage their learning and develop thinking routines, which they can then apply to any content they like. Focusing first on structure means tutors prioritise helping their students become independent. Once students get a handle on how to approach learning, often through internalising 'thinking routines', they can apply these skills to all types of course content.

The elements of tutoring promote metacognitive strategies. Metacognition refers to thinking about thinking, and I explore this term in more detail in Chapter 5. For our purposes here, metacognition is particularly important as access to information becomes more and more ubiquitous. Students can go online with smartphones, tablets and computers almost anywhere and access a wealth of content. Helping students learn to investigate their ideas and think through problems means they can make the most of the internet as a resource rather than focusing on rote learning subject content. Of course, providing subject content support is important, and I explore ways of dealing with content issues in the tutoring toolbox section.

Getting to know the elements of a tutoring session

In this section I start with an example of how a tutoring session might progress based on the position of various elements, so that you can get a sense of how the elements of tutoring can fit together. Then I introduce each of the elements of a tutoring session in more detail and describe what they consist of. After that I provide a facilitation guide as an exercise to train tutors to apply these tutoring elements.

A sample tutoring session

Let's imagine a tutor is having their third maths tutoring session with a student. At the very start of the session the tutor *builds a mini agenda with the student*. In order to build a mini agenda, the tutor might *review work from last week* and ask what the student has worked on during the week at school. In this scenario, the student is working on straight-line graphs and they have a test in a few weeks. The tutor and student decide to spend some time working through some practice questions to see how well the student knows the material. The tutor jots down this mini agenda on a piece of paper (see Appendix 4: Session tracker).

While preparing this agenda the tutor and student *establish an implicit goal* for the session, which is to determine how well the student is able to work with straight-line graphs and practise answering test-type questions. At this stage the tutor *re-establishes the student's expectations* by discussing what grade they would like to get in the upcoming test. The tutor might *disclose some relevant information about themselves* by discussing their own experience learning about straight-line graphs. After the student has had a go *working on course content* by answering some questions, the tutor will have a good idea what the student needs to work on during the week and how well they are progressing towards their goals for the upcoming test.

At this stage of the session the tutor might ask the student to *reflect on prior learning* and consider how much they have learned in the past month. At the end of the session the tutor and student take a few minutes to *determine what to work on next week*.

1. Build a mini agenda with the student

A mini agenda helps keep the tutoring session on track. More importantly, building a mini agenda with the student includes them in establishing control over the session. There are many ways to build a mini agenda with a student. For example, the tutor can simply ask what the student would like to focus on. It is up to the tutor to filter the student's ideas through some practical measure to determine what is possible in a session and what might be most useful. However, they need to make sure that an agenda is built collaboratively and the student can see the value in what it contains.

A tutor may also establish a mini agenda during their first discussions with the student. They can then share this with the student and make sure the student is comfortable with it. In addition, tutors can put items on the agenda for *the next tutoring session.* When there is too much material to cover in one session, or the tutor is not sure how to address a particular issue, some things can be bumped forward to the next session. Demonstrating continuity by moving things forward shows the student that everything they do in tutoring serves a purpose, and it allows the tutor to plan future sessions efficiently.

2. Review work from last week

Reviewing work from last week is a form of reflection. Reviews also help students solidify their learning. There is very strong research supporting *spaced revision* (e.g. Carpenter, 2014), and by reviewing last week's work tutors help students to begin the spaced revision process. A review also gives tutors the opportunity to gauge where the student is at with their learning and what areas may require more work.

3. Establish an implicit or explicit goal for the session

Establishing a goal for the session provides some overarching structure. This may be explicit, such as 'construct a well written introduction to an essay', or it might be implicitly captured within the mini agenda. Either way, a tutor should have some sense of what kind of outcome they expect from the time they have with a student in any particular tutoring session.

4. Establish or re-establish expectations and engagement with them

Earlier I introduced the notion of a sense of agreement. Every tutoring session has opportunities to maintain a sense of agreement. This element of a tutoring session involves maintaining a sense of agreement by checking expectations and the student's engagement with them. Expectations might be related to the work the student will do or the things a tutor will do. Tutors need to make sure they themselves do what they say they will do, as this feeds into student expectations. (Also, the things tutors say they will do usually contribute directly to student learning, such as looking up an answer to a particularly tricky question.)

5. Disclose relevant information about yourself

Anecdotes and drawing on your own direct experience can be a useful teaching tool. However, they can also be confusing. Some tutors and teachers end up focusing too much on themselves, so these anecdotes must be relevant and preferably short. Also, resist the temptation to tell stories to make yourself appear cool or interesting. These types of stories are often ineffective with critical high school students.

6. Work with course content

Working with course content is the last element in the elements of tutoring. During facilitation we often leave this element out so that tutors realise how important all the other elements of a tutoring session are. You can do a lot as a tutor without even touching on content. Of course, content is important, and in the next section I look at specific ways for tutors to work with course content.

7. Reflect on prior learning

Kolb's learning cycle is a well-known model of learning based on experiences, reflecting on those experiences, constructing generalisations about what happens in particular situations, and then entering the cycle again with new experiences. Each time you have an experience, by reflecting on it you can reformulate your generalisations. Through reflecting, people learn more about themselves and are able to apply this knowledge to new or similar experiences.

Often when learning and tutoring we focus on new material. However, time often needs to be spent reflecting on what has been learned previously. Building in time for reflection is important. This can be accomplished using some of the tutoring tools I provide in the next section. A very simple method is to ask the student what they have learned over the past week, month or even year. Reflection is also a great way to take a break during a long session. Some tutors build in reflection every 20 to 30 minutes.

8. Decide what to work on next week

Deciding what to work on next week means students (and tutors) have to:

1. think about what assessments and projects are coming up
2. determine how comfortable they are with the material covered in the current session

3. think about what they will be doing between the current and next session.

These three actions are metacognitive: the student is managing their thinking and learning. Working with a student in the final 5 minutes of a session to determine what to work on next week therefore helps students to develop crucial self-management skills.

Facilitation ideas: Elements of a tutoring session

When training tutors how to use the elements of tutoring, I have found the following exercise to be effective.

Prepare cards with each of the elements of a tutoring session listed on them. Also include up to three or four blank cards. I usually don't provide any explanation of what each element refers to, and this means tutors are forced to discuss them among themselves. After the session you can go into more detail about each element if you like.

Assemble small groups; I have found up to five tutors per group works well. Then, give each group a full set of element cards, some blank cards, a whiteboard pen (to write on blank cards) and some Blu-tack. The task for each group is to put the elements together in the way they would use them in a tutoring session. They can add to the blanks if they think something they would use is missing.

Here is where I leave out the 'work with course content' element. Many groups will add it in; some will not. Also, groups often add new things that have never been thought of before. Groups then stick the elements to a wall or a surface. I am often vague about whether this is a student's first tutoring session or one in the middle of a series.

I try to be very broad in my language so that I do not influence groups to order the elements in a particular way. I even started making the element cards various shapes in an effort to remove any implication that the model should be linear.

After all the groups have put their elements up on the wall or surface, you can ask them to explain why they put them where they did. This is an excellent opportunity to explore tutors' thinking about learning. This exercise can be transformational for tutors, because they realise that their role is as much session management as it is content support—in fact perhaps more so at times. It also gives tutors a comprehensive set of actions to carry out in a tutoring session. Often I find tutors are not quite sure what a tutoring session should entail, and this is the first opportunity they have to see the richness of their role.

The tutoring toolbox: How to work with course content

A large part of tutoring involves helping students master new knowledge. At school, tests and assignments often emphasise content knowledge. As a result, course content is what students are often most concerned about, and what parents often feel their students need to develop. I argue that course content is *not* the most important aspect of tutoring, but it is still a very important part. In practice it is most useful to think of a tight link between course content and metacognitive skills that help students master course content.

In this section I draw on research into student learning and learning in non-school domains to present a toolbox of tutoring techniques that can be applied by tutors to address course content issues. As with the elements of tutoring, the toolbox represents a range of actions that can be applied by the tutor in whatever arrangement suits.

The tutor toolbox contains nine tools. Below I present a brief introduction of each tool. After that I provide some examples of common student issues and consider how the tutoring tools might be applied in these situations.

A toolbox of for tutoring

Demonstrate a process or exercise

There is strong research (see Pashler et al., 2007) to support having students examine worked examples and then answer questions. For example, you could give a student a mathematics question to answer and then show them one that has been done that illustrates the steps involved. After that you can repeat the process, going between the student answering questions and reading through a worked example.

Essentially, the tutor shows the student how to do something, not just by explaining but also by providing a demonstration that includes information about decisions made at each step. Mathematics, physics and chemistry lend themselves well to providing prepared demonstrations in the form of worked examples, but tutors can demonstrate all sorts of things, including how to plan a paragraph or how to structure a long answer. There is an element of modelling here, and a strong tutoring relationship will reinforce a connection between the process or exercise the tutor is modelling and the student's attention.

I would also like to highlight the benefit of *live* demonstration. Live demonstration is much more authentic than explanation. Explanation involves describing an 'ideal' situation. But when tutors demonstrate, they run into problems they have to deal with on the fly, and thus make their thinking visible. The tutor must be confident in their tutoring skills so that they can demonstrate a process or exercise without fear that they might not immediately know the final outcome. Demonstrating a process or exercise in this way results in an authentic experience for the student. If the tutor can value mistakes during a demonstration as feedback, then they will also model a growth mindset.

Lastly, students will often agree with tutors when they ask them if they know how to do something, but often students are not actually that confident with the task. Demonstrating for students helps clear things up when they are either not comfortable asking for help or not sure what help they require. This is also why I say it is important for the facilitator to model the goal-setting conversation in Chapter 2. A goal-setting conversation is usually new to trainee tutors, and so they have no idea how it should go or what questions they might have. Demonstrating provides a model for them and helps them raise questions before they try the conversation themselves.

Give the student a task to do

Novice teachers and tutors often worry too much about what they, as the teacher, will do. They worry about how to explain a complicated idea. They worry that they will not remember the material well enough. They worry about how they will cover everything in the syllabus.

Experienced teachers and tutors know that what they do matters much less than what the students do. Giving a student a task means the tutor can gain a direct understanding of what the student is capable of while also developing the student's skills. If a tutor finds they are talking too much, I always recommend that they give the student something to do. Often the student will benefit much more from working through things themselves than listening to the tutor talking.

Identify a specific problem

When students are struggling with course content it is important to narrow down the issue to something the tutor can deal with. As a tutor it can be hard to understand what a student is struggling with when considering a task in its entirety, especially because the tutor can already do the task. They do not necessarily remember what it is like *not* to be able to do the task. Therefore, zooming in on a specific area helps identify a problem the student can work on. An example might be structuring a paragraph, graphing a linear equation or spelling correctly. Identifying a specific problem provides a starting point for the tutor to focus on. From this point, more challenges will arise over time and these can be addressed in turn.

Determine an initial course of action

Tutors can develop short, medium and long-term plans for student development. If a student presents an issue, often it will not be solved in one tutoring session, in one week, or even in one month. Issues can take a long time to address because learning is holistic, and success at school intersects with a student's entire life.

A useful way I have found when preparing a course of action is to conceive of success at school as a skill. When learning a skill you need to continually practise that skill and apply it. Over time something that was difficult becomes easier, until it becomes part of what you do to accomplish a more difficult or larger-scale task.

For example, when I practise playing the guitar I often struggle to form new chords correctly. A course of action would be to regularly practise the chord shape to a metronome, and then gradually speed up. Over time I will get better and better at the chord shape until it is internalised as part of my guitar playing. Every now and then when I reflect on what I have learned, I realise I can play chords cleanly that previously I could not. I also realise that there are now more advanced things that I cannot do well, and it is these things that I shift my practice focus to.

Similarly, a tutor helps a student to reflect on what they are doing well and what needs work. Some aspects of school work benefit from continual development. For example, writing is a skill that requires ongoing regular practice. An English tutor might therefore ask a student to write a sentence or a paragraph in every session in order to help them develop the skill of writing. Some tutors run mini quizzes at the beginning of each session on things like spelling, vocabulary or basic maths.

Contextualise a specific task within a bigger picture
Learning is a process of constructing an understanding of how things work in the world. This includes tasks at school. I remember struggling to write a paragraph: it simply made no sense to me. I needed to understand how each paragraph was actually different and fitted within the overall structure of an essay.

Initially at school we learned the 'Statement–Elaboration–eXample' model of paragraph writing. When you consider this model you discover it doesn't work for the introduction, it doesn't work for the conclusion, and it is only a loose model when applied to body paragraphs. At the time I did not have this contextualisation, and so I found this paragraph model totally disconnected from the wider role of an essay. As a result I couldn't figure out how to use the model.

This is an example of simplifying a task so much that it separates from the larger task and becomes nonsensical to the learner. Unfortunately, when students show signs of struggling, usually the first response is to hammer them with decontextualised micro-tasks. Continually providing context values a student's ability to understand what they are doing and why. Contextualisation also helps students conquer course content because it provides a framework for them to hang new, or unstable, ideas upon.

In addition, contextualisation highlights the skill aspect of learning. I am happy to practise the same chord shape over and over again on the guitar because I am aware that shifting into that chord cleanly and at speed will mean I can play the song I want to play. Without the song, the practice is a mindless and boring task; with the song, the practice is a definite, exciting progression.

Describe a basic process
Describing a basic process refers to outlining *how* to do something. This might mean planning a paragraph, establishing the points on a graph or spelling a word. Many aspects of course content can be broken down into a process, and it may help a student to understand knowledge as

an *action* rather than as an abstract notion. Describing a basic process is very close to what people traditionally think of when they imagine tutoring or teaching. It is certainly a useful and important part of a tutoring toolbox when applied strategically.

Ask a deep explanatory question

There is a wealth of research (see Pashler et al., 2007) supporting the use of *deep explanatory questions* that encourage students to develop a deep explanatory understanding of key concepts. Deep explanatory questions are by their very nature difficult and tutors should use them judiciously. These are questions that require the student to address causal mechanisms, planning, reasoned arguments and logic. The form of a deep explanatory question will change depending on the subject you are tutoring.

For example, while tutoring history you might ask a question such as, 'What are the causes and consequences of the New Zealand Wars?'. The causes and consequences of historical events are also important for many other subjects, such as economics, media studies and social studies. You could also ask about the motivations of people in certain historical contexts, such as, 'What was the motivation behind Mendel's experiments with peas and inherited characteristics?'. You can probably see how a deep explanatory question goes beyond description and asks students to make connections. Deep explanatory questions will help students reach Excellence level in NCEA. Indeed, at university level students will regularly encounter deep explanatory questions for essay and assignment topics.

In science and maths, deep explanatory questions might ask for scientific evidence for particular theories, or logical justifications for the steps of a mathematical proof. Recent research into physics education carried out at Stanford University and the University of British Columbia (Holmes, Wieman, & Bonn, 2015) involved asking students to continually make and act upon quantitative comparisons between real-world data and physical models. These students were 12 times more likely to make spontaneous comparisons between real-world data and physical models than those in a control group who participated in traditional experimental activities, where they were *not* directed to make comparisons. The test group students were also four times more likely to explain a limitation of a physical model using data. By asking students questions that directed them to compare their real-world data to the expectations of a physical model, the authors were able to help the students develop critical thinking skills crucial to success in science.

The research described above suggests that conducting experiments was not enough for students to explore the relationship between real-world data and a physical model. The students needed to be asked deep explanatory questions to help them develop into critical thinkers. This paper highlights the important role a tutor can play by asking questions.

Assess prior knowledge

Assessing prior knowledge will help tutors diagnose specific issues the student has with course content. Assessing prior knowledge is also a great way to introduce a new topic and to delve more deeply into how well a student has covered previous material. Sometimes students feel comfortable with certain concepts, but once they are asked to express these or work with them you find their understanding is not as comprehensive as it needs to be. Lastly, assessing prior knowledge is a great reflection tool, helping students to establish how far their learning has come and cementing previous learning.

Examples of assessing prior knowledge include a brief quiz, a writing exercise or an analysis task (e.g. identify a theme in a poem). Some tutors I have worked with do a mini quiz at the start of every session. It might include some maths questions, or some factual recall, or a few spelling exercises. Often these quizzes are not difficult, but they can be a great way to cement the basics and make the student comfortable with being continually asked questions.

Give specific descriptive feedback

Feedback helps students learn by identifying a specific area where they can improve their performance. Effective feedback communicates what a student has achieved, and what they need to work on next. Thorough building on previous achievement feedback reinforces a growth mindset by highlighting ongoing development. Tutors should focus on a specific task, emphasise effort, and avoid comparison with others.

In addition, feedback should be connected to criteria. These criteria might come from standards for NCEA, or they might be developed by the tutor and student together (e.g. at a general level during a goals and roles conversation). Going through NCEA standards to identify criteria for good performance is a useful exercise for student development. Alternatively tutors can give feedback on task performance using their own knowledge of the requirements. Ruth Sutton (1995) distinguishes between deep feedback in relation to clear criteria, and impression feedback, in relation to a more general sense of how things are going. I recommend working with both types of feedback.

Applying the toolbox to common student issues

Here is an example of an issue that a student presented, which is relatively common. Christina is doing NCEA Level 1 English. Her goal is to get an Excellence endorsement, but she received a Not Achieved on a recent test essay. She is confused and disappointed because she loves the novel she is writing about and felt that she'd written a great essay in the exam. She had prepared for it extensively in the days leading up to the test. When she gives you the essay you can see straight away that the reason she did not achieve is that the essay is almost totally unstructured. She has an introduction and conclusion, but no body paragraphs. It's just one and a half pages of solid writing. What do you do?

Now I will consider how the tutoring toolbox could be applied to this student's issue. In this case *identifying a specific problem* suggests that Christina has not been able to package her ideas into separate paragraphs. There may be many reasons for this, and if we focus on understanding paragraph structure as an *initial course of action* then hopefully we can address these reasons without needing to dwell on them. We can *assess prior knowledge* through a discussion of essays and paragraphs and then through *giving the student a task to do*. In this case I would ask Christina to write a paragraph, based on her present understanding of a paragraph, in the context of our discussions so far. Then, I may choose this moment to *ask a deep explanatory question* along the lines of, 'If we imagine that newspaper articles are a form of essay, what influences the way the reporter makes their points?'.

After considering this question I would *describe a basic process* of paragraph writing while drawing on our discussions of newspaper articles. This will help to *contextualise a task within a bigger picture*. Then I would ask Christina about an issue she is interested in and a point she thinks is important about that issue. After that I would attempt to *demonstrate a process* of writing a paragraph on that point. Finally, I would give Christina a paragraph writing exercise to do over the intervening period before our next tutoring session (or, if we had time, we could start this exercise during the session). After Christina had completed the paragraph I would *give specific descriptive feedback* relating to the criteria for a well-structured paragraph. From there Christina could identify a specific aspect of paragraph writing to work on to continue to improve.

I hope you can see that this process of using the tutoring tools gives the tutor many different ways to approach an issue related to course content. The tutor's utilisation of each of the tools will inform what happens next, including what tool the tutor chooses to use and how they use it. Tutors will often internalise these tutoring tools, but they are useful to return to so that the tutor has a variety of activities they can turn to when working with different types of students.

Facilitation ideas: The tutoring toolbox

The tutoring toolbox can be taught in a very similar way to the elements of a tutoring session. As with the elements of a tutoring session, prepare a set of cards. On each card list one of the tools from the tutoring toolbox. Also, as before, include up to four blank cards.

Assemble small groups: we have found up to five tutors per group works. Then, give each group a full set of tutoring toolbox cards, some blank cards, a whiteboard pen (to write on blank laminated cards) and some Blu-tack. In addition, give each group a description of a common tutoring issue. I have provided a set of eight student scenarios in Appendix 5 (one of which I have addressed above). The task for each group is to use the tutoring tools to describe how they would help the student address their common tutoring issue. They can add to the blanks if they think something they would do is missing.

This exercise works well with up to 30 participants, with six groups of five, each taking on a different student scenario. You can add more tutoring issues of your own, design a full set of your own and use more or fewer tutoring issues, depending on your group size and the sorts of students the tutors are likely to encounter. After all the groups have decided how to tackle their student problem, ask them to Blu-tack the tools they used to the wall, and then get them to describe to the group what they have done.

This exercise is an excellent way to help tutors gain confidence that they will be able to address a wide range of student issues using some relatively simple tools. During the elements exercise, tutors identified a place for the element *work with course content*. As a result they can see how they can fit the tutoring toolbox into the overall tutoring session.

A comprehensive model of tutoring

This chapter outlines the two central aspects of a tutoring session: the structural elements that make up the tutoring session and the tutoring tools that tutors apply to address student issues with content. Combined with the tutoring relationship, a comprehensive model of tutoring emerges.

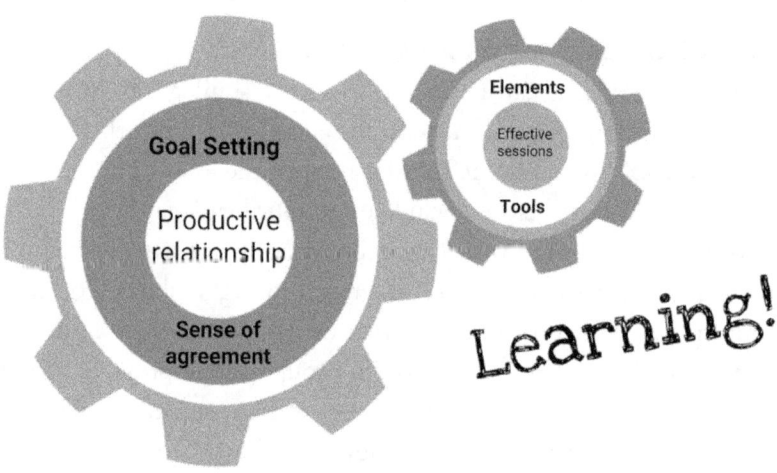

Figure 2: A model of tutoring

I have found that tutors are very comfortable with the concept of building a tutoring relationship as a basis for delivering effective tutoring sessions. In addition, the elements of tutoring and tutoring tools ensure that tutors know what they are actually supposed to *do* in a tutoring session. Often new tutors are nervous that they will not have enough work to go over, or are simply confused about what actually happens in a tutoring session. The model depicted above, and described in Chapters 2 and 3, can be used to demonstrate an overview of what happens in tutoring.

Chapter 3 Summary: Key points about tutoring tools and techniques

- It's useful to think of tutoring sessions as being made up of 'content-free' elements that help students explore their own learning, and tutoring tools which address specific course content issues.
- The elements of a tutoring session provide structure for student learning, and include things like reflecting on prior learning, preparing a mini agenda for the session and (re)establishing expectations (see p. 35).
- The tutoring toolbox includes a range of tools that tutors can use with students to address specific issues with course content. Tools include techniques like *demonstrate a process or exercise, identify a specific problem* and *describe a basic process* (see p. 36).
- Eight student scenarios are provided in Appendix 5 which facilitators can use to train tutors to apply the tutoring tools to a real complex student issue.

Chapter 4 Case studies

Many different groups are interested in helping students in their communities to do better. These groups include schools, community groups and iwi organisations. Every context for education is different, and so in this chapter I present four case studies from different groups, describing how they have decided to use tutoring to help students in their community.

I begin with two examples from schools engaged in traditional peer tutoring programmes, where older students help younger students. Next, I explore a community-based homework centre supporting the Afghan community, run by an Afghan university student and drawing on the support of friends and family. Lastly, I consider an iwi-based programme focused on building higher-level competence for the management of a forestry resource. The two school programmes have been running for many years, the community-based programme has only been running for a year, and the iwi programme is still being set up. Exploring these programmes as they make decisions at different stages of their development will help you consider the organisation and focus of your own programme.

Traditional school peer tutoring

Peer tutoring programmes are common in schools. From my research I have found that these programmes have relatively similar structures, with a head teacher in charge and input from a lead group of students. Here I discuss the peer tutoring programmes of two large New Zealand secondary schools. After presenting both case studies I provide my assessment of how these programmes could improve.

Epsom Girls Grammar School

Epsom Girls Grammar is an all-girls school based in central Auckland. It is a large decile 9 school with 2,200 students, and it has a strong academic and social reputation. Its peer tutoring programme has been running for at least 10 years.

Organisation and resources

The programme is led by Sue, the head of mathematics, although peer tutoring is available for all subjects. A student committee deals with the day-to-day running of the programme. This committee is made up of Year 13 students, and each year a new committee takes over. There is some carry over of systems, but each new committee changes the way things are done.

The peer tutoring committee have a computer available to track the tutors and students participating in the programme. However, they use a paper-based system to match up tutors and students. Students who want peer tutoring fill out a form and place it in a box in the library. The student committee then matches tutors to tutees and sends a slip of paper to both the tutor and tutee, who then make contact with one another and start tutoring.

Tutoring is informal and generally content-focused. Extra materials are not usually required as students utilise materials provided in class or they independently source their own materials. The school provides a room for tutoring, and tutors and students meet during lunch or after school. Typically tutors use the room that is available, although sometimes they will tutor elsewhere. Sue's primary role is to support the student committee. She photocopies forms when they run low, and the school purchased the computer the student committee members use to keep track of students and tutors.

Recruiting tutors

Tutors are recruited at assembly. Year 13 students speak about the programme and its benefits. The school does not always have enough tutors, especially for high-demand subjects such as mathematics. Tutors do not receive any financial reward, but there are awards for the tutors providing the most tutoring. There is no training provided for tutors.

Obstacles

The main obstacle is communication. The slips of paper are not always reliable. Sometimes people do not turn up to their tutoring sessions. At exam time tutoring stops because tutors have their own exams to focus on.

Newpark Boys High School[1]

Newpark Boys is a decile 10 school. It is a large school with over 2,000 students and a strong academic and social reputation.

Organisation and resources

The Newpark peer tutoring programme is organised by the head of the Learning Support Department. This department's staff work specifically with students at risk of not progressing through assessments. At times learning support staff use the peer tutoring programme in addition to more specific learning support, or for students who are not deemed high risk. Students not participating in learning support can also attend the programme.

The programme is run in the old gym, which has been turned into three rooms and can fit about 100 students. Generally about 50 to 60 students attend the tutoring programme, once a week during lunch times. Tutees are paired with a senior student and are usually Years 9 or 10. Tutors are not provided with any additional materials and work with what is provided as part of the class curriculum.

The programme was previously be administered by six lead prefects, but there was a lack of accountability. Now a secretary runs the administrative side of the programme, documenting attendance and tutor and tutee details. However, the prefects still play a part in running the programme; for example, they help match up students to tutors. Because prefects know the students well they can select matches that are likely to be successful. Prefects take a roll during tutoring times, and they put up notices and publicise the programme around the school.

Recruiting tutors

The tutors are senior Year 12 and 13 boys who apply to be part of the programme. Newpark never has trouble recruiting tutors. Students like to help, and they can add participation in the programme to their

---

1 The name of the school has been changed.

CV. The tutors all get up on stage at some time during the year, and recognition and fulfilling a desire to help are the primary outcomes for the tutors. Also, students hoping to be a prefect expect it to strengthen their application.

The head of Learning Support meets with the boys who want to tutor at the start of the year, but there is no specific training. The programme is run relatively informally and focuses on helping students with course content issues. Students will often eat lunch together during tutoring, so there is a relationship aspect to the tutoring, but tutors are not trained in how to utilise the tutoring relationship as part of tutoring.

Obstacles

The main obstacle Newpark faces with its peer tutoring is having tutors available during senior exam time. Unlike at Epsom Girls Grammar, Newpark attempts to continue the peer tutoring during exams. However, senior students will be away from the school on study leave during the lead up to younger students' exams, and so for that period they have few tutors available. One solution to this problem is to invite the stronger Year 10 boys to tutor during this time, although that solution is not ideal as the boys are inexperienced tutors.

Traditional school peer tutoring: Discussion

In this section I consider some avenues for developing the way peer tutoring programmes are run in schools. The two case studies I presented above are representative of peer tutoring programmes in schools, and I draw primarily on these case studies and broader discussions I have had with teachers.

Administration

Peer tutoring programmes require some administration in terms of recruiting students to participate as tutees and also as tutors. Rooms need to be organised, attendance may need to be tracked, and resources need to be provided. In some cases outcomes may be tested too. While administration may seem relatively minor, it can quickly become overwhelming and discouraging for a teacher in charge.

Overall, the administration required to run a peer tutoring programme is related to the goals of the programme. Often administration can be minimised through establishing clear goals for the programme and then ensuring that any administration is tightly linked to programme goals. For example, spending considerable time tracking attendance might not be required for many programmes. Perhaps a general sense of uptake can serve the goals of the programme. Other programmes may want to carefully track attendance, along with the change in grades from the previous year. If this is the case, then there should be clear reasoning for gathering such data—and *suitable resourcing*. Even in a perfect scenario, where each student can provide this information, there is considerable administration involved in collating the data, let alone analysing it. Clarifying what data are required in order to support the ongoing development of the programme will determine the level of administration required.

In the case studies above, one of the schools had administrator support while the other relied on either a head teacher or a student committee to deal with administration. In the latter case the programme will inevitably be more informal in terms of data collected. In the former case, when an administrator is available additional data can be collected.

Working with student committees

Student involvement in the leadership and administration of peer tutoring programmes helps establish buy-in from students, both as tutors and as tutees. However, student committees change each year, and their quality and engagement will fluctuate. Therefore strong leadership is required from a head teacher. Preferably clear processes are in place. However, students will also want to develop their own way of doing things. Encouraging student ownership of the tutoring programme without reinventing the wheel each year requires a head teacher to guide the committee through regular meetings to develop the administration of the programme effectively.

Newpark positions the peer tutoring programme within Learning Support. While they work with a student committee, the Learning Support staff deal with the administration of the programme. This model ensures continuity of the programme and does not rely too heavily on one teacher, or on a changeable student committee.

Tutor training
None of the programmes I spoke with had training in place for tutors. This is a major issue and one this book seeks to rectify. The lack of training will limit the potential value of peer tutoring and will most likely neglect the processes involved in tutoring that go beyond content support. Often people believe that pairing a student who achieved good grades with a younger student will result in a positive outcome. However, this is not always the case. While peer tutoring is not an overly difficult activity, learning some key processes and approaches is the difference between a successful programme and a mediocre one.

At one of our training sessions a tutor called Jack continually gave answers that suggested he was not quite grasping the tutoring model. Jack focused on telling the student what to do and then waiting for them to do it. After the training we decided to sit down with Jack and explore his model of tutoring because we felt he was not ready to begin tutoring. It turned out that he was a successful student and had often asked his father for help. His father had told him what he needed to do to answer a question and then left him to it. This was the same model of tutoring that Jack used. This model was so strongly embedded that the training was ineffective for him. While this raises some issues about the effectiveness of training for large groups, my point here is that when people first tutor they default to whatever educational model they think will work. Too often this model involves telling a student what to do and then waiting for them to do it. If success in education and life were this simple then this book would be far shorter.

I recommend a half-day training programme for tutors based on the material in Chapters 2 and 3. Half a day is enough to cover the training material, although if administrative material (i.e. how the programme works) needs to be covered, then an extra hour might be required. Careful observation of tutors is enough to ensure that tutors are mastering the material, especially during moments such as the initial session role-play (see p. 11), and during group work on tutoring elements and the tutoring toolbox (p. 36). Many times we have seen tutors dominate their group, and this has raised concerns for us regarding how inclusive this tutor will be when working with a student. A dominant tutor may not always be an issue, and often they are strong academically, but we will end up pairing those tutors with confident, high-achieving students seeking to push themselves.

This observation process can continue during peer tutoring sessions, especially when they occur in a specific room at a school. In essence, the tutoring model detailed in this book provides a benchmark for activities that student committees and head teachers can expect to see in peer tutoring sessions.

Resources

I always recommend that tutors initially rely on the resources that students have received in class. Most schools are very good and provide students with everything they require to cover course material. However, school-run peer tutoring programmes also have an opportunity to provide some additional material for tutors and students to work through. For mathematics, physics, chemistry and similar subjects a bank of exam questions with some worked examples would be very useful. For subjects that are usually assessed with long-answer or essay-based questions, a similar bank of questions with some answer outlines or full answers could be provided. These types of question banks are often put together by textbook publishers, and many teachers already have a collection of their own.

Community homework centre

Community groups seeking to support students can establish homework centres with varying levels of organisation. Sometimes they just provide a space and time for students to gather; at other times they provide more specific subject support. In this section I consider a relatively new homework centre run by Salva Shah in the Afghan community.

The Homework Centre

The Homework Centre has been running for 1½ years. The centre was established by Salva Shah. Salva is an architecture student and an experienced one-to-one tutor for high school students. She established the centre after noticing that many parents in the Afghan community do not have a good understanding of how the New Zealand school system, and particularly NCEA, operates. This was not really an issue with course content, but rather with understanding how course content is assessed and what is required of school students. As a result parents found it difficult to support their children with school work. Salva noticed that students were disengaged and not doing well at secondary school. With University Entrance grades becoming more challenging to attain, many Afghan students were missing out on future education opportunities.

Organisation and resources
Salva established a community tutoring centre on Sundays at a local school. The school offered a room for them to use for a small fee. Recently they have been able to move to a school that does not charge any room hire fees. The centre runs for 4 hours. During the first 2 hours Salva works with younger students at primary and intermediate level. During the second 2 hours Salva works with high school-level students. The approach is a combination of group and individual work. Salva sees a large part of her role as providing knowledge about how school works that parents do not have good access to.

She asks students to pay what they can, and some pay $5 or $10 while others cannot afford to pay anything. Salva's mother drives to pick up and drop off some students who cannot travel to the school. Salva provides some textbooks that she has collected from various sources, and sometimes provides worksheets for students.

Recruiting tutors
Salva has recruited some university friends to act as tutors. In addition, some of the high school students arrive early to help the younger students. A local tutoring company provides training for Salva's tutors, and they also have the option to take up some private tutoring for the company.

Obstacles
Salva struggles for time and financial resources. As a Master of Architecture student she has significant projects to work on, so she relies on the support of her family, community members and tutors she has recruited to participate in the programme. Financially their needs are relatively modest, but it would be useful to be able to provide some stationery for students, to reimburse her mother for petrol costs, to pay for photocopying, and to provide textbooks and a collection of past exam and assessment questions. Also, paying tutors an hourly rate

would help recruit tutors to work in the centre. At the time of writing Salva was in the process of applying for community grants to assist the centre.

Iwi-based tutoring programme

Many iwi, iwi organisations and smaller hapū- and marae-based groups seek to improve educational outcomes for students in their whānau. In this case study I focus on a comprehensive programme of educational development in a region outside of the main centres and consider the unique issues which larger programmes like this face.

The Forestry Management Education Programme

The Forest Management Education Programme is under development, and therefore provides a useful case study for people making decisions about the purpose and structure of their peer tutoring programme. This case study focuses on a North Island iwi whereby a number of Māori land block titles were consolidated in the 1960s. These blocks formed over 35,000 hectares of planted forests for the beneficial owners and their descendants. The Crown was the tenant of these lands and its lease expires over the next 5 to 10 years.

In preparation for the expiry of the leases, the Māori-owned trusts are preparing for taking over the management of their lands. The Forest Management Education Programme recognises that the owners do not currently have the capacity to fully self-manage the forestry resource. Building a capability model in forest management is important to these landowners, who are kaitiaki (guardians) of their resources. This means developing young people to ensure they have the necessary skills to manage the resource.

A major advantage iwi groups have is their long-term perspective. In the case of the Forest Management Education Programme, the plan has a significant timeframe of about 20 years, and this plan fits within larger strategic goals of the Māori-owned forest trusts. The programme aims to develop the capacity within the iwi to manage the resource, and this means assisting young people on a pathway towards completing forest qualifications through the Forestry Schools at Lincoln University and Waiariki Institute of Technology. Of course, many students may begin the programme and decide not to study forestry management. However, the programme aims to help ensure students finish school with the science, technology, engineering and mathematics (STEM) skills that give them the opportunity to enter into a wide range of careers.

Programme structure

The programme includes holiday programmes for younger students and parents, during which they will explore science. These programmes are primarily a fun introduction to STEM subjects through things like robotics and chemistry experiments. Students from 8 to 13 years participate in these holiday programmes.

Older students at high school level will participate in a peer tutoring programme. I will explore the challenges in setting up this programme in more detail below. After high school, students will be encouraged to apply for scholarships through the Māori-owned forest trusts. Lastly, the community will be engaged to promote the value of a career in forestry management, and the importance to tino rangatiratanga (self-determination) of developing the competence required to manage tribal resources.

Peer tutoring programme structure

The iwi's rohe (territory) includes several schools, most of which are low decile. Decisions about where to focus the programme need to be made, and initially a small town has been the focus for a pilot for the peer tutoring programme. There is a tutoring centre in a larger city nearby, but the travel to the city and the costs associated are prohibitive. Also, the iwi is interested in developing internal capability, which means having control over the tutoring provision.

The programme will first work with students who are owners and/or descendants of beneficial owners of the forestry trusts. Because it will be based in a small town without a university there is not a large group of potential tutors available. Recruiting and training older students to tutor younger students was not practical in this scenario, and so an outside provider was chosen to provide trained tutors to deliver tutoring. Tutoring will be delivered over Skype, and the iwi will organise necessary arrangements to support the students. Students will travel to Auckland to meet their tutors in person, to help establish the tutoring relationship. Students are expected to have one session per week during terms 3 and 4, with additional sessions as required. Students and tutors will be able to stay in touch also via text message and phone, so students can ask questions whenever they need to.

In the long term some of the students receiving tutoring in this pilot group will develop into tutors themselves. Over time the programme aims to become self-sufficient and not rely on outside tutors.

Obstacles

Using Skype for tutoring presents a challenge because tutors and students can find it more difficult to build a relationship over Skype. Computer-mediated communication can be less personal, and since the tutor isn't physically present there can be less incentive for the student to engage in the tutoring session, or even to attend. The iwi is addressing this issue by taking students to Auckland to spend a few days with their tutors. During these few days the tutors and students will spend time together, attend science workshops and visit universities. Tutors will also be trained in specific techniques to use when conducting Skype tutoring.

Another key obstacle is the need to align several large organisations. This programme requires the largest resourcing of all the programmes described here, and that resourcing comes from various funding organisations. The programme therefore requires strong visionary leadership, with good relationships across these funding organisations. In the case of this programme this leadership comes from a contracting organisation which is managing the programme on behalf of one of the trusts. It's important to take small steps, and demonstrate success, so that other funders can be convinced to come on board. This is more of an administrative and management issue than a tutoring issue, but it demonstrates how important the overall management of a tutoring programme is. This situation also suggests that the various strands of the programme will require additional administrative resourcing in order to report outcomes to each of the funding organisations with a vested interest.

With larger programmes such as this one, aligning many different groups will often pose a significant challenge. Ensuring there is a clear vision, starting conversations early and good reporting back to funding providers will help smooth the process.

Case studies: Concluding thoughts

In this chapter I have explored four different tutoring programmes. The high school based programmes are both similar with mainly structural differences in terms of where each programme is positioned, and how it is managed. The community homework centre and the iwi-based tutoring programme are quite different examples, with large differences in scope. The community homework centre has very little access to resources, while the iwi-based tutoring programme has the potential to access significant resources. Although a certain level of resourcing is required, I observed that a lead group or individual energising the programme was most important to its ongoing success.

People setting up or running tutoring programmes of their own will be able to learn from the ways these programmes have decided to operate in their particular contexts. Running a tutoring programme of any size is primarily about leadership. Clarity of purpose will ensure the often limited resources are spent in areas that are required and the programme is successful in helping tutors and students develop their skills.

A final note on evaluation is important here. Evaluating the success of a tutoring programme can be complex. You may think that evaluating a change in grades from one year to another would be a simple calculation, but in practice this is very difficult. There might not be a clear comparison subject from one year to another, students may take a more ambitious programme in a particular year, and it may be difficult to convince students to give you their grades. Furthermore, tutoring provides outcomes that go beyond an increase in grades, and these outcomes might not become visible within one year. My preference is to collect data on student numbers, including number of sessions and regularity of attendance. This data can show the size of the programme and any growth. Student surveys can show the value students place on their tutoring, and can uncover benefits from tutoring beyond an increase in grades.

Chapter 4 Summary: Key points about setting up tutoring programmes

- A clear vision is required, especially when working with student committees, institutional processes, volunteer tutors or multiple funding organisations.

- Tutor training is highly recommended as often tutors are volunteers, or inexperienced.
- For a basic and successful tutoring programme the primary commitment is time. Financial requirements can be modest, and community grants and sponsorship can cover these costs.
- Carefully consider the level of administration required in a tutoring programme. Administration can be limited by ensuring that only information that is definitely required for funding or evaluation is collected.
- At the same time, for any tutoring programme to grow some benefits must be demonstrated. Collecting feedback from students or numbers of participating students can help show the usefulness of a tutoring programme.

Chapter 5 Delving into the literature

In this chapter I explore academic research in four areas that are central to tutor training: emotional safety, student agency, goal setting, and metacognitive skills. I begin with emotional safety, because relating is so crucial to tutoring. After that I consider student agency, focusing on establishing a practical definition for agency in tutoring. Then I explore goal setting. Tutors who artfully integrate goal setting into their sessions can be very effective, while those who treat goal setting in an overly functional or prescriptive manner can be quite damaging. Finally I consider metacognitive skills. These competencies help people to apply themselves to whatever challenges arise, and research is showing the importance of metacognitive competencies to wider societal outcomes.

Emotional safety: Why relating well matters

The tutoring model I advocate highlights the importance of the tutoring relationship. Everyday experience suggests that strong relationships are an important prerequisite for success at school, and research supports this experience. In an influential article on social relationships and motivation, Wentzel (1998) shows that students with strong relationships with their peers pursue goals more strongly. Wentzel's work also shows that strong relationships with teachers predict both interest in school and positive goal pursuit.

Despite findings illustrating the importance of relationships in schools, the complex social environment that schools operate within means that strong relationships are not always present. For example, bullying has a powerful negative effect on emotional safety and students' ability to relate to one another. Many school reform efforts seek to improve social relationships. Juvonen (2007) reviews a range of literature on such school reform efforts, especially those that facilitate positive social relationships to increase student engagement. She highlights the importance of emotional safety and peer relationships to support students to relate well to their school community. Beyond emphasising the importance of positive relationships, I would like to suggest that for both peer tutors and tutees, peer tutoring programmes present an excellent way for schools to promote positive relationships and stimulate a culture of support and educational striving.

No clear guidelines have emerged regarding building an emotionally safe school experience, and interventions continue to be developed. For example, a recent study by Gehlbach et al. (2016) investigated how sharing similarities between teachers and students affected relationships and grades. In the study, teachers and students were told of interests and traits they shared with one another. As a result, teachers and students thought more highly of one another and built stronger relationships. Importantly, there was a positive effect on student grades when students related well to their teachers. While interventions like this show positive effects, the aforementioned complexity of a school's social environment and wider societal environment can make research-based interventions difficult to implement in all schools. Interventions are always likely to be school-centred, requiring careful application by the school community. Gehlbach et al.'s work highlights the importance of positive relationships and suggests one way that teachers and students can build relationships through sharing similarities.

Beyond emotional safety I argue that strong relationships provide a powerful force of reciprocity, and this force can be utilised to set high expectations. If students do not have a strong relationship with their tutor or teacher, then that person's expectations are less likely to be of much importance to the student. Snipes, Fanscali and Stoker (2013) point out that there is significant research suggesting students perform well when teachers set high expectations. While a causal link has not been established between expectations and student performance, a programme evaluated by Wallberg and Kahn (2011) which encouraged high expectations and student rights, showed an increase in student engagement and participation. Based on this work, and practical experience, I encourage setting high expectations. The tutoring relationship can be used as a way to encourage students to strive to meet these expectations.

Neuroscience provides strong support for relating well and for the importance of emotions for learning. In Chapter 2 I use the metaphor of the brain as a garden fertilised by emotional safety. Immordino-Yang (2015) points out that emotions are not just powerful motivators of learning but that people can only think deeply about things they care about. It is much easier to find out what people authentically care about when you have a strong relationship with them. Immordino-Yang's book *Emotions, Learning, and the Brain* provides an excellent educator-centred examination of the role of emotions in learning.

The evidence I present here investigates relating well from both a psychological perspective and a neuroscientific perspective. These studies support what we already know from everyday experience: feeling emotionally safe and relating well to those around us provide a positive space for learning. However, the research gives us more detail with which to explore this everyday sense. In addition, research gives educators the evidence they need to purposefully take time to nourish strong relationships.

Student agency: The importance of giving (and taking) control

In Chapter 2 I introduced the concept of student agency. Agency can be defined in many ways and has deep theoretical and philosophical roots in a variety of fields. Here I start with the idea that agency relates to the notion of selfhood and the ability to initiate actions and instigate events (Bruner, 1996; Linell, 1998). Educators generally want to promote agency, because if a student can initiate an action then they are well on the way to learning to produce that action by themselves. In my own research I suggest that producing an action with ownership over that action is a useful way to define successful learning (Pirini, 2015). In this section I explore how agency is used in the literature and develop an understanding of agency that has a practical aspect, which teachers, tutors and students can use during tutoring and training.

Agency is often discussed in the education literature but is not clearly defined. The lack of a clear definition makes it difficult to develop a deeper theoretical and methodological understanding of agency. Despite this, the education literature points towards several ideas regarding agency that align with practical tutoring skills.

In his article "Mindsets and Student Agency", Briceno (2013) argues that effective teaching should be about developing positive mindsets in students. Schools should move away from seeking performance on demand in the form of tests and assignments, and instead should seek to develop students who possess and maintain positive mindsets. Briceno identifies four such mindsets, including a growth mindset. While he does not define agency clearly, he equates positive mindsets with increased student agency.

Briceno's notion of positive mindsets aligns with developing the non-cognitive competencies discussed later. These competencies help students to manage and assess their own learning. For example, imagine a student who has a clear sense of their learning outcomes and how they are progressing towards them. This student has agency in terms of initiating and controlling actions towards the outcome.

In a similar vein, Perkins, Tishman, Ritchhart, Donis and Andrade (2000) advocate helping students to identify the intellectual opportunities that exist in everyday encounters. They argue that students have been conditioned through schooling to focus on a narrow abilities-centric view of intelligence. Most educators have probably experienced students asking 'Will this be in the test?' This type of question indicates a learner focusing on assessment, which in some ways is an act of metacognition and self-management, but in other ways limits the learner to a narrow understanding of a topic. This type of assessment-focused learning is discouraged in schools, yet the need to rank thousands of students inevitably encourages narrow quantitative assessment.

Perkins et al. (2000) argue that educators should foster intellectual curiosity, creativity and open-mindedness. In order to develop these traits, students are tasked with identifying opportunities to apply their skills rather than being directed. We can see that providing less direction may lead to students expressing agency over their own learning. Indeed, Perkins et al. use the term 'mindfulness' to refer to an open state of curiosity, and contrast this with 'mind-lessness', which is associated with a fixed view of the world. As with Briceno, Perkins et al. relate agency to mindsets, and suggest a close relationship between positive and open mindsets and student agency.

Another important area in the literature regarding agency is the way students interact with objects. Tishman and Palmer (2007) argue that using artistic objects fosters curiosity and open-minded exploration. They suggest that since art is complex it requires a personal interpretation rather than seeking a 'correct' interpretation. Therefore when students engage with art they are forced to explore their own experience rather than move towards a correct answer.

However, in my own research I have found that simply engaging with an object, such as an artwork—or indeed with any object—is not necessarily enough to foster agentive engagement with that object. A sociocultural perspective of the world suggests that people's interactions with objects are permeated by social forces. These forces influence how people interpret and act with objects, and are therefore important mediators of interactions with objects.

Researchers exploring how people move through art galleries have shown that people mostly engage first with the interpretation of the art before they engage with the art itself. From Tishman and Palmer's perspective these people are seeking some guidance about the correct way to interpret art prior to experiencing it. Similarly, I recall sitting in my English class waiting for my teacher to tell me what themes we were supposed to analyse in a book. I want to suggest that regardless of the type of material or object we are engaging with (whether art, a novel or a mathematics problem set), our sociocultural environment plays a key role in influencing the manner of our interaction and the extent to which we are agentive.

Tutors can help students to engage agentively in their studies, and that is why tutors need to have a practical understanding of agency. Ritchhart and Perkins (2008) suggest that educators should encourage students to make their thinking visible through using questions such as 'What makes you say that?' or 'What do you think you know about topic/object x?' They argue that these types of questions encourage students to reflect on the basis of their own thinking. Returning to the sociocultural perspective, I would like to suggest that these types of questions help students to explore aspects of the sociocultural environment they are positioned within. Through this exploration students have the opportunity to accept, reject or adjust to established practices. This means the tutor's role is not simply to help the student to engage in the world, but also to encourage active reflection on that engagement.

My own work on agency (Pirini, 2015) develops theoretical/methodological tools for the analysis of agency and aligns with giving students control over objects and their environment, while simultaneously encouraging them to take control or ownership. My findings suggest that this process can require careful management, as sometimes students actively express agency, and at other times may appear to be agentive and yet further analysis reveals they are relying heavily on the guidance or direction of the tutor.

Overall the literature on agency requires further theoretical and methodological development. This is an area I am particularly interested in and actively working in. From a practical perspective my findings and the literature support encouraging students to engage in their environment physically (e.g. through handling objects such as the "Courses and Goals Sheet", or developing their own materials, or controlling the location of the tutoring session), and through questioning their interpretations of the world and their own actions within this world (e.g. 'Why do you think that?').

Goal setting: Why there is no best way

In Chapter 2 I discussed the "Courses and Goals Sheet" and how it can be used to frame a conversation about goals. However, although I refer to goals, I am careful to focus on the way that a conversation about goals establishes a *sense of agreement*, which can be returned to as required.

I am cautious about focusing too strongly on goals because students all set goals differently. As discussed earlier (see p. 13), asking tutors to line themselves up from 1 to 10 on a scale of 'engagement in goal setting' illustrates this difference. Once tutors are able to approach goal setting from a considerate and open place, then the literature relating to goals can be treated as exploratory rather than prescriptive.

In the goal-setting literature the term 'goal pursuit' is used to include both committing to a goal and implementing steps to achieve that goal.

One important aspect of successfully achieving goals that is highly relevant to tutoring is the student's ability to self-regulate. Two strategies (with considerable support in the literature) to improve self-regulation are *mental contrasting* and *implementation intentions*. Once tutors have established a strong tutoring relationship they may like to experiment with some of the techniques below to help students develop self-regulation skills.

Mental contrasting

Mental contrasting involves imagining a possible future and then thinking about obstacles that might exist. This can be quite an enjoyable process, and I address some ways of stimulating mental contrasting in Chapter 2 during the goal-setting conversation. These include questions such as 'What would it be like if things were a little bit better?' and 'What might you see if you achieved that?'.

Oettingen, Wittchen and Gollwitzer (2012) point out that mental contrasting is energising: people become excited about their prospects for the future. In addition, when using mental contrasting people create links between a possible future, obstacles to that future and the behaviours required to overcome those obstacles. For example, imagine a student desiring an Excellence in English who decides that excessive Facebook use is an obstacle to this goal.

It is important to note that mental contrasting requires some desire for the outcome or some positivity associated with it. Trying to convince a student they should pass English is unlikely to produce the required positive emotions if they do not already exist. Here we can see the importance of a tutoring relationship in helping the student to develop emotional engagement with subjects that might at first seem uninteresting. A tutor who knows their student well might be able to link English to a topic or outcome the student is more emotionally engaged in.

In the courses and goals conversation I suggest talking about the previous year and trying to explore what the student would like to improve. I once set a goal with a student of feeling more relaxed when walking into their exams. Again, I want to emphasise the artfulness of goal setting. One area of the literature that is lacking is an articulation of how the action of mental contrasting could be stimulated by another person, such as a tutor, teacher or coach.

Lastly, mental contrasting has been shown to support *feasible goals*. In studies of students using mental contrasting, those who had a high expectation of success committed significant effort to goal pursuit. Those who did not have high expectation of success did not commit significant effort. Thus, those goals that were more feasible (i.e. had a high expectation of success) were pursued; those that were less feasible (i.e. low expectation of success) were not pursued.

The notion of feasible goals is too extensive to explore in detail here, but it is clear that the notion of *feasible* is highly subjective. What matters with feasibility is not the objective feasibility of the goal but the subjective feasibility; that is, the feasibility of the goal for the person setting it. Again, this requires some artful exploration of goals by a goal setter, and I argue that a tutor can support this exploration by building on the basis of a strong relationship.

Implementation intentions

Implementation intentions have been shown to be a very effective tool to pair with mental contrasting (Locke & Latham, 2012). Implementation intentions are often phrased as 'if … then' sentences. For example, let's return to the student carrying out a mental contrasting exercise where they visualise a future where they gain Excellence for English. They then switch to thinking about their current reality. This student knows they will need to do work in the evenings to prepare for their English assignments, and they realise that Facebook distracts them. An implementation intention such as 'If I am working on the computer, then I will disable Facebook chat' might be able to help them overcome this obstacle.

Stanford researcher B. J. Fogg (2009) has an excellent goal-setting programme related to implementation intentions called Tiny Habits. Fogg's approach emphasises coupling small changes in lifestyle to current habits. One example I played with in my own life was saying, 'After I pour hot water into my coffee pot, I prepare a snack to take to work'. Eventually my snacks turned into making my lunch and purposefully shopping for food that I could take to work with me. I now buy my lunch far less frequently than before and have a range of food available to take for lunch at home.

Both the Tiny Habits approach and implementation intentions

work to couple changes in behaviour to a person's current situation. This approach makes a lot of sense because we do not always act with awareness of what we are doing. Many of our behaviours are routine or habitual. Implementation intentions and Tiny Habits work with our current routines and habits to introduce new behaviours.

Coupling implementation intentions with mental contrasting has support in the literature (Oettingen, Wittchen, & Gollwitzer, 2012). You can probably see quite clearly how imagining a new future, contrasting it with the current reality to identify obstacles and then setting implementation intentions go together well. In the courses and goals conversation tutors focus on mental contrasting. However, over time tutors might like to introduce some implementation intentions or Tiny Habits.

Beyond test performance: Metacognitive competencies

In Chapter 2 I introduced the concepts of a growth mindset and grit. Here I provide links to further reading on these two key concepts by positioning them within the broader category of metacognitive competencies.[1]

One way to think of metacognitive competencies is as all the things that happen outside of content-focused actions, such as writing a paragraph, analysing the themes in a text or answering a maths question. Metacognitive competencies include time management strategies, assessing your own performance and developing strategies for success. Taylor (1999) provides the following definition of metacognition:

> appreciation of what one already knows, together with a correct apprehension of the learning task and what knowledge and skills it requires, combined with the agility to make correct inferences about how to apply one's strategic knowledge to a particular situation and to do so efficiently and reliably. (Taylor, 1999, p. 37)

---

1 Metacognitive competencies are also referred to as non-cognitive competencies, and as mindsets, essential skills and habits (MESH) (Gabrieli, Ansel, & Bartolino Krachman, 2015). I treat these terms as interchangeable, although not all researchers agree. However, for my purposes here the definition I draw on from Taylor (1999) is sufficient. I prefer to use the term 'metacognitive competencies' because MESH is an unwieldy acronym and 'non-cognitive competencies' suggests that these skills do not involve cognition, when they certainly do.

These competencies are not merely peripheral. Research shows that students who have strong metacognitive competencies do better in standardised tests (Snipes, Fancsali & Stoker, 2013).

A model offered by Snipes et al. (2013) demonstrates how metacognitive competencies influence performance on assessment. The model (Figure 3) illustrates how academic mindsets and learning strategies (types of metacognitive competencies) intersect with academic behaviours such as attending class and engaging in class, and learning outcomes such as performance on a test.

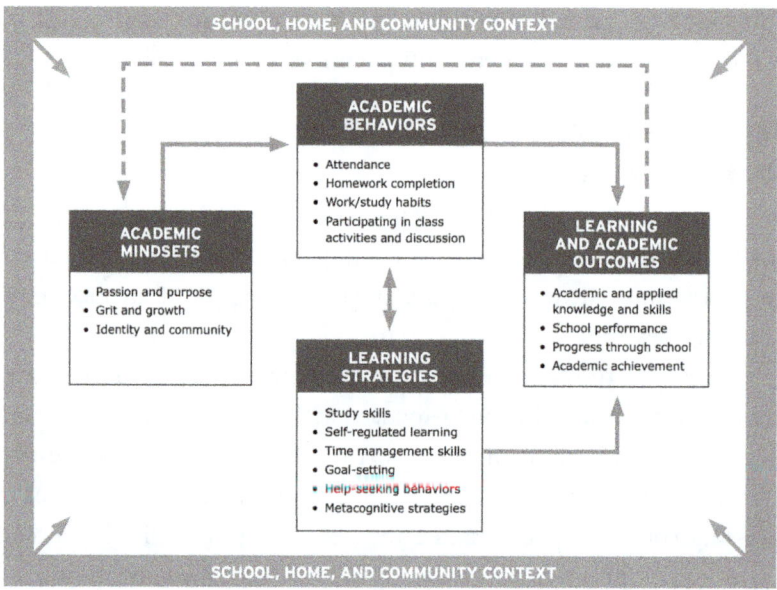

Figure 3: The links between various components of school success (Snipes et al., 2013).

Earlier I mentioned that a student told me they pay more attention in class because of their tutor. This is one small example of tutoring supporting academic behaviours, and I would like to suggest that more work is required in this area using a qualitative approach. Quantitative measures of performance on assessments do not capture the more nuanced outcomes from one-to-one tutoring support.

Importantly, the model in Figure 3 includes the school, home and community context. Students who are in difficult contexts where resources are limited and physical and emotional safety are not guaranteed are likely to struggle with academic mindsets, learning strategies and academic behaviours. Of course the result is a downstream impact on learning and academic outcomes. Snipes et al. (2013) emphasise that the school, home and community context, including peer interaction, has a major influence on interventions targeting metacognitive skills.

Further work is needed to assess the societal contexts that students operate in and to establish what sort of support is effective. I am especially interested in the ways that peer interactions influence the way that students perceive and produce their identities as learners. A well-structured and well-supported peer tutoring programme may be one way to encourage positive peer interactions relating to learning.

In addition to success at school, metacognitive competencies are beginning to be linked to wider societal outcomes more strongly than standardised test performance. A study carried out in Dunedin provides some of the core evidence supporting the importance of one of these metacognitive competencies: self-control. The Dunedin Longitudinal Study[2] began in 1973 and included 1,037 children born within a 12-month period. Participants have since been assessed 13 times. The study has become famous for its rigorous data collection and the success researchers have had in keeping over 90% of participants involved since the study began.

At each data collection point participants spend a day with researchers participating in various tests. Self-control is one of the measures that researchers used with participants when they were between the ages of 3 and 11 years. Since then researchers have linked participants with high self-control to several outcomes, including financial position, health and low criminal conduct. Researchers argue that interventions addressing self-control might therefore promote prosperity and reduce societal costs from welfare, health care and law enforcement (Moffitt et al., 2011).

Metacognitive competencies are applicable to any challenge faced in life. Although there is still a strong focus on standardised testing in schools, more emphasis is now being placed on metacognitive competencies. Tutoring shows great promise in helping both student and tutor to develop metacognitive competencies.

---

2   The study's full title is the Dunedin Multidisciplinary Health and Development Study.

How to improve metacognitive skills

Extensive work has begun on interventions to improve metacognitive competencies in schools and among school-aged children. Snipes et al. (2013) provide an excellent review of mindset interventions. They point out that while a lot of work is being done, studies often focus on one kind of skill and no studies have achieved any kind of scale. Interventions that work when supported extensively by researchers who provide a lot of time and analytical attention to the intervention may not work nearly as well when schools are left to implement the intervention alone.

I argue that the tutoring programme I describe here supports the development of metacognitive competencies. Specifically, students develop a caring, respectful relationship with a tutor, who carefully offers opportunities for autonomy and challenge while helping the student to find a wider context or meaning for the tasks they tackle in school. Tutors communicate high expectations while supporting students to consider their own contribution to success and to develop grit and a growth mindset.

Studies of peer tutoring and metacognition indicate that peer tutoring programmes are effective in helping both tutors and students to improve their metacognitive competencies. King (1998) showed that tutoring partners could use a questioning protocol to mediate each other's learning. Tutoring partners would question, explain and problem solve together. They would also monitor and regulate each other's learning. King provided a relatively simple questioning protocol for students to use together, and she claims that due to the social construction of knowledge this questioning protocol helped students to explore their thinking. The type of questioning protocol King used has been further expanded upon by the *making thinking visible* movement (Richhart & Perkins, 2008).

Shamir, Zion and Spector-Levi (2008) have shown the importance of training students in tutoring skills. Shamir et al. randomly placed students into either an experimental group or a control group. The experimental group was trained in a peer tutoring programme which highlighted metacognitive skills while the control group received a general preparation course. In the experimental group both tutors and tutees exhibited higher levels of critical thinking on subsequent tests.

In a similar study, this time with university students, De Backer, Van Keer and Valcke (2012) showed that students participating in a reciprocal peer tutoring programme used more metacognitive strategies in comparison with control groups. De Backer et al. asked students to solve problems while verbalising their thinking process. Those students who had participated in the peer tutoring programme took more care to orient themselves to the task, monitor their progress and self-evaluate.

Clearly the literature supports working with other people to improve metacognition. In addition, when engaged in peer tutoring, training is important. Providing tutor training that embeds metacognitive competencies helps both tutors and students in subsequent tests.

Chapter 6 Conclusions

In Chapter 1 I introduced the remarkable results Cameron achieved working with Sean Buck. The following chapters discussed the two key components of effective tutoring that Cameron utilised to help Sean: the tutoring relationship, and tutoring tools.

The tutoring relationship highlights the importance of relating well, modelling grit and a growth mindset, and drawing on reciprocity. More broadly the tutoring relationship positions tutoring within family, community and school. The tutoring relationship is central because education is one part of a complicated life that students are navigating as they mature. This creates a messy environment where the right option is not always clear.

Research on mindsets, grit and metacognition supports broadening our focus on what is required to succeed in education to take a more holistic perspective. Although teachers are highly aware of this, students often take quite an instrumental focus to school work, seeking only to get good marks. Whether this is an outcome of the institutional environment or something else is beyond the scope of this book. What I would like to highlight is that peer tutors are likely to focus on helping students get good grades, and to do that by tutoring them in the way that they assume tutoring is done. Often, this 'natural' approach reinforces an instrumental test and exam focus. Training tutors to value the relationship aspect of learning means tutors can put time and effort into relating well. Chapter 2 gives tutors some approaches achieving this. These include setting goals with a student focus, and modelling the more ethereal aspects of learning such as mindsets.

The tutoring tools section of the book gives tutors some guidance around the overall structural elements of a tutoring session. The elements training is often the section of our tutor training where students really start to 'get it'. They see that there is a lot to tutoring which is not about course content, and the elements exercise on p. 43 illustrates this effectively. The elements section of the training is also the moment where tutors who were nervous about how to actually work with students start to see some options opening up for them.

The tutoring toolbox is where tutors start to work with course content, and this is purposefully presented after relationship work, and larger structural elements of a tutoring session. These tools were developed from practical experience and reviews of the literature. Tutors will always have something to try if they become familiar with a range of tools. Applying just one of the tools can open up a pathway to useful progress in a tutoring session. Many of the tutoring tools are reasonably intuitive, but it is the combination of many tools that gives tutors confidence to work with a range of students.

The case study section of the book provides examples of different ways that schools, a community group, and an iwi group are trying to improve educational outcomes. Context is hugely important in education, and many initiatives that work in one area might not work in another. This is a central issue with educational research. It's also why I believe that supporting groups to implement their own educational programmes is likely to have the largest impact. These groups know their context, they know the people they want to help and they have the passion to find solutions. Often what they don't have is access to good research translated into practical approaches. This is the gap that this book addresses.

There is strong support in the chosen literature for the type of tutor training I advocate throughout this book. Specifically, the literature highlights the importance of:
- strong, meaningful relationships between educators and students
- promoting student agency through helping students to explore their thinking
- setting goals by imagining a better future and then considering present obstacles
- improving metacognitive competencies through peer interaction.

The tutor training programme draws upon research on education, business coaching and neuroscience. At the same time, the programme is practical, accessible and carefully structured through tools such as the "Courses, Goals and Roles Sheet" (Appendix 1). The facilitation guides throughout are designed to help people to implement their own tutor training.

The effectiveness of training is notoriously difficult to assess, and I prefer to focus on implementing tutor training and then continuing to monitor outcomes and improve training for the specific school context. This book establishes a foundation for great tutor training, and further work during implementation and evaluation will ensure that schools, community groups and iwi groups develop a tutoring programme that meets their needs.

Appendix 1 Courses, Goals, and Roles Sheet

The Courses, Goals, and Roles Sheet is discussed in detail in Chapter 2, p. 14. I advise tutors to work through a sheet like this with every student as early as possible in the tutoring relationship.

Courses, goals, and roles

Name:

Courses:
1.
2.
3.
4.
5.
6.
7.

Goals for the year:
1.
2.
3.

Roles and expectations:

Appendix 2 Goals and Roles conversation script

The Goals and Roles conversation script is used in combination with the Courses, Goals, and Roles Sheet (Appendix 1) discussed in Chapter 2. This conversation script can be used during facilitation to help guide tutors first learning to talk about goals and roles with a student.

Goals and Roles conversation script
There are many different types of goals and ways of bringing up goals with tutees. Here's one formula you could try. Or, you could pick out certain aspects of this and use them in your own way.

1. Ask a general question about how school is going. Aim to get a narrative about how things are, what is good, what is not so good.
   - What would it look like if it were just a tiny bit better?
   - What would it look like if it were a little bit better?
   - What would it look like if it were a lot better?
   - What would it look like if it were perfect?
2. Gather more details with questions like these:
   - Why do you want to achieve this goal?
   - Where do you think this goal will lead to?
   - What will a goal like this help you do?
   - What is involved in achieving this goal?
3. The essential outcome is to create a real sense of a better future, and that the student chooses goals for themselves. At this stage you might be able to **ask the student** to write down one, two or three key goals.
4. You might like to suggest a mix of process goals (e.g. I will do 3 x 20 minutes of maths homework a week) and outcome goals (e.g. I will get a Merit endorsement).

Roles and expectations
Building on this vision of the future, you can now discuss how tutoring can help the student get there. You might start with the following questions:

1. What do you think I can do to help you reach these goals?
2. What do you think you might need to do to reach these goals, and how can I help you do that?

Lastly, contribute your own ideas about how the tutoring sessions can operate. Ask the student to take a few notes regarding roles and expectations on the Courses, Goals and Roles sheet.

Moving on ...

At this stage, I suggest moving on to finding out how organised the student is and what their capabilities are. Here are some suggestions:

1. Ask about what assessments they have for the year, when these are and how they feel about each of them.
2. Ask about their study habits, time management and organisation of school material (notes, etc.).
3. Do a small test of their ability or knowledge, or ask to see a sample of work.

Appendix 3 Grit Scale

The Grit Scale is discussed in Chapter 2, p. 28. It was developed by Duckworth et al. (2007) and provides a measure of perseverance and persistence towards long-term goals. I prefer to use the Grit Scale to frame a conversation around perseverance. Tutors could do the Grit Scale in their own time, or use it during training.

12- Item Grit Scale

Directions for taking the Grit Scale: Please respond to the following 12 items. Be honest – there are no right or wrong answers!

1. I have overcome setbacks to conquer an important challenge.
    - ❏ Very much like me
    - ❏ Mostly like me
    - ❏ Somewhat like me
    - ❏ Not much like me
    - ❏ Not like me at all

2. New ideas and projects sometimes distract me from previous ones.*
    - ❏ Very much like me
    - ❏ Mostly like me
    - ❏ Somewhat like me
    - ❏ Not much like me
    - ❏ Not like me at all

3. My interests change from year to year.*
    - ❏ Very much like me
    - ❏ Mostly like me
    - ❏ Somewhat like me
    - ❏ Not much like me
    - ❏ Not like me at all

4. Setbacks don't discourage me.
    - ❏ Very much like me
    - ❏ Mostly like me
    - ❏ Somewhat like me
    - ❏ Not much like me
    - ❏ Not like me at all

5. I have been obsessed with a certain idea or project for a short time but later lost interest.*
    - ❏ Very much like me
    - ❏ Mostly like me
    - ❏ Somewhat like me
    - ❏ Not much like me
    - ❏ Not like me at all

6. I am a hard worker.
    - ❏ Very much like me
    - ❏ Mostly like me
    - ❏ Somewhat like me
    - ❏ Not much like me
    - ❏ Not like me at all

7. I often set a goal but later choose to pursue a different one.*
    - ❏ Very much like me
    - ❏ Mostly like me
    - ❏ Somewhat like me
    - ❏ Not much like me
    - ❏ Not like me at all

8. I have difficulty maintaining my focus on projects that take more than a few months to complete.*
    - ❏ Very much like me
    - ❏ Mostly like me
    - ❏ Somewhat like me
    - ❏ Not much like me
    - ❏ Not like me at all

9. I finish whatever I begin.
    - ❏ Very much like me
    - ❏ Mostly like me
    - ❏ Somewhat like me
    - ❏ Not much like me
    - ❏ Not like me at all

10. I have achieved a goal that took years of work.
    - ❏ Very much like me
    - ❏ Mostly like me
    - ❏ Somewhat like me
    - ❏ Not much like me
    - ❏ Not like me at all

11. I become interested in new pursuits every few months.*
    - ❏ Very much like me
    - ❏ Mostly like me
    - ❏ Somewhat like me
    - ❏ Not much like me
    - ❏ Not like me at all

12. I am diligent.
    - ❏ Very much like me
    - ❏ Mostly like me
    - ❏ Somewhat like me
    - ❏ Not much like me
    - ❏ Not like me at all

Scoring:

1. For questions 1, 4, 6, 9, 10 and 12 assign the following points:
   5 = Very much like me
   4 = Mostly like me
   3 = Somewhat like me
   2 = Not much like me
   1 = Not like me at all

2. For questions 2, 3, 5, 7, 8 and 11 assign the following points:
   1 = Very much like me
   2 = Mostly like me
   3 = Somewhat like me
   4 = Not much like me
   5 = Not like me at all

Add up all the points and divide by 12. The maximum score on this scale is 5 (extremely gritty), and the lowest scale on this scale is 1 (not at all gritty).

Duckworth, A.L., Peterson, C., Matthews, M.D., & Kelly, D.R. (2007). Grit: Perseverance and passion for long-term goals. *Journal of Personality and Social Psychology, 9*, 1087-1101.

Appendix 4 Session tracker

The session tracker is discussed in Chapter 2 on p. 32. This sheet can be introduced during training, and I like to demonstrate how a tutor might use this to track what they do in a session, and what they might do next session. The sheet helps tutors to minimise their planning, and reflect on prior tutoring sessions.

Session tracking sheet

Student name:

1. Date:	
Covered this session:	Plans for next session/actions:
2. Date:	
Covered this session:	Plans for next session/actions:
3. Date:	
Covered this session:	Plans for next session/actions:

4. Date:	
Covered this session:	Plans for next session/actions:

5. Date:	
Covered this session:	Plans for next session/actions:

6. Date:	
Covered this session:	Plans for next session/actions:

7. Date:	
Covered this session:	Plans for next session/actions:

8. Date:	
Covered this session:	Plans for next session/actions:

Appendix 5 Student issue scenarios

These student issue scenarios are discussed in Chapter 3, p. 43. During tutor training students can design a tutoring session using the tutoring tools to address one of these scenarios.

Scenario 1
Christina is doing NCEA level 1 English. Her goal is to get an Excellence endorsement, but she received a Not Achieved on a recent test essay. She is confused and disappointed, because she loves the novel she is writing about and felt that she'd written a great essay in the exam. She had prepared for it extensively in the few days leading up to the test. When she gives you the essay, you can see straight away that the reason she did not achieve is that the essay is almost totally unstructured. She has an introduction and conclusion, but no body paragraphs; it's just one big 1½ page block of solid writing. What do you do?

Scenario 2
Connor wants to get a Merit or Excellence endorsement for his NCEA level 1 maths, and is putting quite a lot of work in but is really stuck at a level of basic understanding. This is especially true of his work in the tables, equations and graphs unit. He is very comfortable reproducing the basic formula at achieved level, but is struggling to make the connections between these formula and lines on a graph that students need to understand in order to reach a higher grade. He is very frustrated because he's working hard and, naturally, does not understand what he doesn't understand. What do you do?

Scenario 3
Simon really wants to go to medical school. He achieved NCEA Level 1 science last year with no endorsement. You are tutoring him for Level 2 biology. He did not achieve his recent practice exams. He also told you that physics and chemistry are not going very well either, but he is still determined to get top grades. He doesn't know why his grades are so far from his goal, because he loves science and in junior high school he barely had to put any work in. He also does reasonably well in his science internals. Basically, he has a lot of ground to make up to reach his goal, and at least one major part of his learning and/or study habits is not working. What do you do?

Scenario 4

Victoria is a very bright student doing NCEA Level 3 and Scholarship English. Last year, she achieved great results throughout the year but missed out on her subject endorsement because she got Achieved for her exams. This was a big blow and she doesn't want to repeat it. You have seen essays and assignments she has written for homework and in class, and they are excellent. She calls herself a perfectionist and it is clearly reflected in her work. Her teacher told her recently that her perfectionism might be what is hindering her from performing well in exams, because he doesn't understand why her performance is so inconsistent. What do you do?

Scenario 5

Carmen wants to get straight Excellences for Level 1 science. She loves science and aims to study human biology at university. She even enjoys studying for science exams, and achieved Excellence in nearly all of her recent prelims. Maths and English are more difficult though. She knows she'll need good maths grades to keep up with science as she progresses through to Levels 2 and 3, but she doesn't enjoy the subject and feels lost in class. She finds algebra especially hard and recently received unhelpful feedback from her teacher when she asked for help, which left her feeling even more helpless in maths classes. She is having similar problems in English. She tells you she is studying *To Kill a Mockingbird* and doesn't really understand it, but feels too embarrassed to say so in class. You are tutoring her for maths and English, 2 hours per week, until her exams in 6 months' time. She is reluctant to set goals. What do you do?

Scenario 6

Arie is a high performing Year 12 student studying a mixture of NCEA Levels 2 and 3 subjects. You are tutoring him for Level 3 and Scholarship biology. His understanding of course content is very solid, even this early in the year (late term 1). He tells you he recently quit sports (swimming and rugby league) in order to study, which he now does for 2 hours every afternoon and a half day every weekend. His parents confirm this. Arie wants to focus his tutoring sessions on learning to answer those high-level NCEA and Scholarship questions with complex terms such as 'demonstrate comprehensive understanding,' 'analyse,' and 'critically evaluate' in the questions and marking criteria. He understands the dictionary definitions of these words but is not sure how to go about performing them in exam conditions. What do you do?

Scenario 7
This year, Jade needs to get NCEA Level 2, literacy, and a Merit subject endorsement in maths in order to start the electrician's apprenticeship she wants to do next year. She's currently at Achieved level for most of her subjects but knows she needs to put more work in before exams begin. You're tutoring her for maths and Jade recently told you she has stopped going to maths classes because she doesn't see the point. She thinks she can get to Merit level on her own before exams in 6 weeks. You're not sure about that as she hasn't achieved Merit before and doesn't seem very aware of good study skills, but you can see that her confidence is fragile, so you need to proceed with caution. What do you do?

Scenario 8
Dylan is studying for NCEA Level 2 and wants to study design at an Australian university after high school. He works hard at art and graphics, gets great grades, and has almost finished his big final assignments for art, graphics, and media studies. Exams are in 4 weeks and he has barely started studying for his externals: maths, English, general science, and media studies. He knows he'll need to get good grades for University Entrance but is very resistant to studying. You're tutoring him for English and maths but you can see he needs help with study skills. He has never made a study plan before and is very disenchanted by the study techniques his teachers have suggested (reading over notes, etc.). He struggles to sit for extended periods of time and concentrate on reading or writing. He is currently at half and half Achieved/Not Achieved level for his achievement standards in his subjects aside from visual arts. What do you do?

References

Alton-Lee, A. (2003). *Quality teaching for diverse students in schooling: Best Evidence Synthesis Iteration (BES)*. Ministry of Education. Retrieved from https://www.educationcounts.govt.nz/publications/series/2515/5959

Briceno, E. (2013). Mindsets and student agency. *Unboxed: Journal of Adult Learning in Schools, 10*, 107–115.

Bruner, J. S. (1996). *The culture of education*. Cambridge, MA.: The President and Fellows of Harvard College.

Carpenter, S. K. (2014). Spacing and interleaving of study and practice. In V. A. Benassi, C. E. Overson, & C. M. Hakala (Eds.), *Applying the Science of Learning in Education: Infusing psychological science into the curriculum* (pp. 131–141). New York, NY: American Psychological Association.

Credé, M., Tynan, M. C., & Harms, P. D. (2016). Much Ado About Grit: A Meta-Analytic Synthesis of the Grit Literature. *Journal of Personality and Social Psychology*. Retrieved from http://www.academia.edu/25397556/Much_Ado_about_Grit_A_Meta-Analytic_Synthesis_of_the_Grit_Literature

De Backer, L., Van Keer, H., & Valcke, M. (2012). Fostering university students' metacognitive regulation through peer tutoring. *Procedia—Social and Behavioral Sciences, 69*, 1594–1600. doi.org/10.1016/j.sbspro.2012.12.104

Duckworth, A. L., Peterson, C., Matthews, M. D., & Kelly, D. R. (2007). Grit: Perseverance and passion for long-term goals. *Journal of Personality and Social Psychology, 92*(6), 1087.

Duckworth, A. (April, 2013). *Angela Duckworth: The power of passion and perseverance* [Video file]. Retrieved from https://www.ted.com/talks/angela_lee_duckworth_grit_the_power_of_passion_and_perseverance

Dweck, C. (2006). *Mindset: The New Psychology of Success*. New York, NY: Random House.

Fogg, B. J. (2009). A behavior model for persuasive design. In *Proceedings of the 4th International Conference on Persuasive Technology* (p. 40). ACM. Retrieved from http://dl.acm.org/citation.cfm?id=1541999

Gabrieli, C., Ansel, D., & Bartolino Krachman, S. (2015). *Ready to be counted: The research case for education policy action on non-cognitive skills* (Working paper No. 1.0) (pp. 1–31). Boston, MA. Transforming Education.

Gehlbach, H., Brinkworth, M. E., King, A. M., Hsu, L. M., McIntyre, J., & Rogers, T. (2016). Creating Birds of Similar Feathers: Leveraging Similarity to Improve Teacher–Student Relationships and Academic Achievement. *Journal of Educational Psychology, 108*(3), 342–352.

Holmes, N. G., Wieman, C. E., & Bonn, D. A. (2015). Teaching critical thinking. *Proceedings of the National Academy of Sciences, 112*(36), 11199–11204. doi.org/10.1073/pnas.1505329112

Immordino-Yang, M. H. (2015). *Emotions, learning, and the brain: Exploring the educational implications of affective neuroscience* (1st ed.). New York, NY: W. W. Norton & Company.

Juvonen, J. (2007). Reforming middle schools: Focus on continuity, social connectedness, and engagement. *Educational Psychologist, 42*(4), 197–208. doi.org/10.1080/00461520701621046

King, A. (1998). Transactive peer tutoring: Distributing cognition and metacognition. *Educational Psychology Review, 10*(1), 57–74.

Lambert, L. (2002). Toward a deepened theory of constructivist leadership. In D. Walker, D. P. Zimmerman, J. E. Cooper, M. Lambert, M. Gardner, M. Szabo, & L. Lambert (Eds.), *The constructivist leader* (2nd ed.). New York, NY; Oxford, OH: Teachers College Press.

Linell, P. (1998). *Approaching dialogue: Talk, interaction and contexts in dialogical perspectives* (Vol. 3). Amsterdam: John Benjamins Publishing Company. Retrieved from http://www.jbe-latform.com/content/books/9789027285492

Locke, E. A., & Latham, G. P. (2012). *New developments in goal setting and task performance*. London, UK: Taylor and Francis.

MacFarlane, A., Glynn, T., Cavanagh, T., & Bateman, S. (2007). Creating culturally-safe schools for Maori students. *Australian Journal of Indigenous Education, 36*, 65–76.

McCaleb, M., & Mikaere-Wallis, N. (2005). Relationship-shaping: Teacher consistency and implications for brain development. *Education, 7*(2).

Moffitt, T. E., Arseneault, L., Belsky, D., Dickson, N., Hancox, R. J., Harrington, H., et al. (2011). A gradient of childhood self-control predicts health, wealth, and public safety. *Proceedings of the National Academy of Sciences, 108*(7), 2693–2698. doi.org/10.1073/pnas.1010076108

Mueller, C. M., & Dweck, C. S. (1998). Praise for intelligence can undermine children's motivation and performance. *Journal of Personality and Social Psychology, 75*(1), 33.

Oettingen, G., Wittchen, M., & Gollwitzer, P. (2012). Regulating goal pursuit through mental contrasting with implementation intentions. In E. A. Locke

& G. P. Latham (Eds.), *New developments in goal setting and task performance* (pp. 523–548). New York, NY: Routledge.

Pashler, H., Bain, P. M., Bottge, B. A., Graesser, A. C., Koedinger, K., McDaniel, M., & Metcalfe, J. (2007). *Organizing instruction and study to improve student learning.* Washington, DC: National Centre for Education Research, Institute of Education Sciences, U.S. Department of Education. Retrieved from http://ncer.ed.gov

Pekrun, R., Goetz, T., Titz, W., & Perry, R. P. (2002). Academic emotions in students' self-regulated learning and achievement: A program of qualitative and quantitative research. *Educational Psychologist, 37*(2), 91–105. http://doi.org/10.1207/S15326985EP3702_4

Perkins, D., Tishman, S., Ritchhart, R., Donis, K., & Andrade, A. (2000). Intelligence in the wild: A dispositional view of intellectual traits. *Educational Psychology Review, 12*(3), 269–293. doi.org/10.1023/A:1009031605464

Pirini, J. (2015). *Research into tutoring: Exploring agency and intersubjectivity.* Unpublished doctoral thesis, AUT University, Auckland.

Ritchhart, R., & Perkins, D. (2008). Making thinking visible. *Educational Leadership, 65*(5), 57–61.

Ritchhart, R., Church, M., & Morrison, K. (2011). *Making thinking visible: How to promote engagement, understanding, and independence for all learners.* San Francisco, CA: Jossey-Bass.

Shamir, A., Zion, M., & Spector-Levi, O. (2008). Peer tutoring, Metacognitive processes and multimedia problem-based learning: The effect of mediation training on critical thinking. *Journal of Science Education and Technology, 17*(4), 384–398. doi.org/10.1007/s10956-008-9108-4

Snipes, J., Fancsali, C., & Stoker, G. (2013). *Student academic mindset interventions: A review of the current landscape.* San Francisco, CA: IMPAQ International.

Sutton, R. (1995). *Assessment for Learning.* Salford, UK: RS Publications.

Taylor, S. (1999). Better learning through better thinking: Developing students' metacognitive abilities. *Journal of College Reading and Learning, 30*(1), 34–45. doi.org/10.1080/10790195.1999.10850084

Tishman, S., & Palmer, P. (2007). Works of art are good things to think about. In *Conference proceedings: Evaluating the Impact of Arts and Cultural Education Conference.* Paris: Centre Pompidou. Retrieved from http://www.visiblethinkingpz.org/VisibleThinking_html_files/07_Whats_New/WorksOfArt.pdf

Tomlins-Jahnke, H., & Mulholland, M. (2011). *Mana tangata: Politics of empowerment*. Wellington: Huia Publishers.

Wallberg, P., & Kahn, M. (2011). The Rights Project: How rights education transformed a classroom. *Journal of Childhood Studies, 36*(1), 31–35.

Wentzel, K. R. (1998). Social relationships and motivation in middle school: The role of parents, teachers, and peers. *Journal of Educational Psychology, 90*(2), 202–209.

Winitana, M. (2012). Remembering the deeds of Māui: What messages are in the tuakana–teina pedagogy for tertiary educators? *MAI Journal, 1*(1), 29–37.

Index

accountability of students 17
administration of tutoring programmes 47, 48, 53, 55–56, 58
agency, student 13, 16–17, 18
    see also self-management and self-regulation by students
    research 61–64
agreement *see* sense of agreement
Alton-Lee, Adrienne 16–17
art, student engagement with 63
assessment 15, 17, 21, 34, 48
    see also NCEA (National Certificate of Educational Achievement)
    bank of exam questions with worked examples 52, 53
    focus on 62
    influence of metacognitive competencies 62, 68
    mindset and grit 22, 25
    multiple assessments and assignments 10
attention in class 2

Blackett, Emma 5
bullying 60

cancellation of tutoring 18
community, home and school contexts 9, 29, 52–53, 55, 68–69, 73
community homework centre 52–54
conscientiousness 26
contexts, school, home and community 9, 29, 52–53, 55, 68–69, 73
contextualisation 39, 42, 73

course content, working with 34, 36, 44
    see also tutoring toolbox
Courses, Goals and Roles Sheet 10–11, 75
critical thinking skills 41

deep explanatory questions 40–41, 42
demonstration of a process or exercise 36–37
Duckworth, Angela Lee 26–27
Dunedin Longitudinal Study 69
Dweck, Carol 4, 22, 24–25

elements of a tutoring session 4–5, 30–31, 44, 73
    elements
        build a mini agenda with the student 32–33
        decide what to work on next week 34–5
        disclose relevant information about yourself 34
        establish an implicit or explicit goal for the session 33
        establish or re-establish expectations and engagement with them 33
        reflect on prior learning 34
        review work from last week 33
        work with course content 34, 36, 44
    facilitation ideas 35–36
    key points 45
    sample tutoring session 32
emotional security 3, 7
    research 59–61
engagement of students 16–17, 33
    Afghan students 53

with art 63
maintaining a sense of
  agreement 33
and mental contrasting 65
and positive social relationships 60
sociocultural influences 63–64,
  68–69
Epsom Girls Grammar School peer
  tutoring programme 47
  obstacles 48
  organisation and resources 47
  recruiting tutors 47
evaluation of tutoring programmes 57,
  58
exam stress 13
expectations
  establishing or re-establishing 33
  importance in educational
    achievement 3, 8
  maintaining a sense of
    agreement 33
  and tutoring relationship 60–61

facilitation ideas 74
  elements of a tutoring session 35–
    36
  goals and roles conversation 13–15,
    37
  tutoring toolbox 43–44
failure
  fear of 3, 25
  fixed mindset 4, 22–23, 25
  growth mindset 4, 22
feedback
  deep feedback 42
  impression feedback 42
  praise for effort rather than
    talent 4, 25
  specific descriptive feedback
    41–42, 43

fixed mindset 4, 22–23
  comparison with growth
    mindset 24
Forestry Management Education
  Programme 54–55
  obstacles 56
  peer tutoring programme
    structure 55–56
  programme structure 55
framework for students to work
  within 30–31
funding of tutoring programmes 53–
  54, 56, 57, 58

goal pursuit 64, 65
goal setting 11, 12, 44, 72
  research 64–67
  using a line-up to demonstrate goal-
    setting behaviour 13
goals
  see also motivations of students
  context and purpose for
    tutoring 11
  feasible goals 66
  perseverance in pursuing long-term
    goals 4, 26
  procedural goals 12
  school peer tutoring
    programmes 50
  for tutoring sessions 33
goals and roles conversation 10–12, 18
  built on growth mindset
    approach 25, 26
  facilitation ideas 13–15, 37
  goals and roles conversation
    script 15
  guide to carrying out an effective
    discussion 12–13
  and mental contrasting 65

purpose 12
real-play using goals and roles
   conversation script 14
script 76–77
grit 4, 19–22, 26–28
   see also metacognitive strategies and
      skills
   Grit Scale test 28–29, 78–81
growth mindset 4, 19–23, 29, 62
   see also metacognitive strategies and
      skills
   attribution of success 25–26
   comparison with fixed mindset 24
   influencing development in
      students 24–26

holistic nature of education 9
home, school and community
      contexts 9, 29, 52–53, 55,
      68–69, 73
Homework Centre 52–53
   obstacles 53–54
   organisation and resources 53
   recruiting tutors 53

implementation intentions 66–67
iwi-based tutoring programme 54–56

knowledge *see* prior knowledge
Kolb's learning cycle 34

Lambert, Linda 7–8
leadership in tutoring programmes 57
learning
   see also prior knowledge
   effect of stress 3, 7
   importance of emotions 7, 61
   reflecting on prior learning 34
   student agency 61

student agency and
   engagement 16–17
Lezac, Jason, mindset and grit
   example 19–22

mana 9
mental contrasting 65–66
mentoring 8
metacognition, definition 67
metacognitive strategies and skills 31,
      35, 36
   interventions to improve skills 70–
      71
   research 67–69
Mikaere-Wallis, Nathan 7
mindsets
   see also fixed mindset; growth
      mindset
   interventions to improve
      metacognitive skills 70
   and student agency 62, 63
mindsets, essential skills and habits
      (MESH) 67
   see also metacognitive strategies and
      skills
mini agenda 32–33
mini quizzes 41
motivations of students
   see also goals
   and effective tutoring 2
   exploring in a goals and roles
      conversation 12
   external 3

NCEA (National Certificate of
      Educational Achievement)
   Afghan students 52–53
   example of the effect of tutoring on
      grades 1–2

standards, as criteria for good performance 41, 42
Newpark Boys' High School peer tutoring case study 48
  obstacles 49
  organisation and resources 48, 50
  recruiting tutors 48–49
non-cognitive competencies *see* metacognitive strategies and skills
Nugent, Dean 30

obligations to tutors, influence on students 3, 7, 8, 9, 29
Olympic Games, 2008, mindset and grit example 19–22

paragraph writing 39, 42, 43
passion 4, 26, 27
peer interactions of students 59–60, 69
peer tutoring *see* tutoring
peer tutors *see* tutors
perseverance 4, 22, 26, 27, 29
personality traits 27
power relationships 9
praise
  for effort rather than talent 4, 25
  influence on development of a growth mindset 25
prior knowledge
  assessing 41, 42
  reflecting on 34

questioning protocol for tutoring partners 70

real-plays 14
reciprocity
  tuakana–teina concept 8–9
  in tutoring relationship 3, 7–8, 9

recruitment of tutors 47, 48–49, 53, 54
reflection 33, 34, 41
relationships in schools 59–61
  see also tutoring relationship
research literature
  emotional safety 59–61
  goal setting 64–67
  metacognitive competencies 67–71
  student agency 61–64
resilience 26
resources for tutoring 47, 48, 50, 52, 53, 57
  see also funding of tutoring programmes
reviewing previous week's work 33
role models, peer tutors as 8

scenarios, student issues 43–44, 85–87
school, home and community contexts 9, 29, 52–53, 55, 68–69, 73
school peer tutoring programmes
  administration 47, 48, 49–50
  discussion 49–52
  Epsom Girls Grammar School 47–48
  goals 50
  Newpark Boys' High School 48–49, 50
  promotion of positive relationships 60, 69
  resources 47, 48, 50, 52
  student committees 47, 50
school social relationships 59–61, 68–69
science, technology, engineering and mathematics (STEM) skills 55
self-control 69

self-management and self-regulation
   by students
   see also agency, student
   assessment-focused learning 62
   determining work for next tutoring
      session 34–35
   implementation intentions 66–67
   mental contrasting 65–66
sense of agreement 16–17, 33, 44, 64
   built on growth mindset
      approach 25, 26
   example conversation 17–18
session tracker 32, 82–84
setbacks, responses to 19, 22, 27, 28, 29
Shah, Salva 53–54
Skype, for tutoring delivery 55–56
SMART goals 12
sociocultural influences on
   students 63–64, 68–69
spaced revision 33
Statement–Elaboration–eXample
   model of paragraph writing 39
stress
   effect on learning 3, 7
   exam stress 13
student committees 47, 50
student issue scenarios 43–44, 85–87
success
   fixed mindset 4, 25–26
   goal pursuit 66
   growth mindset 4, 19–23, 25
   links between components of school
      success 68
supervision 8

teaching, metaphor of plumbing and
   electrics in a house 30
thinking

critical thinking skills 41
   making thinking visible 31, 63, 70
   reliance on emotional security for
      higher-level thinking 7, 61
   Think Puzzle Explore routine 31
time commitment in tutoring
   programmes 53, 58
time management 10, 15, 67
Tiny Habits 66, 67
training of tutors 47, 49, 51–52, 53, 58, 70, 71, 72, 73–74
tuakana–teina concept 8–9
tutoring
   see also community homework
      centre; iwi-based tutoring
      programme; school peer tutoring
      programmes
   cancellation 18
   comprehensive model 44–45
   and development of metacognitive
      skills 70–71
   example of effect on NCEA
      grades 1–2
   key components (*see* elements
      of a tutoring session; tutoring
      relationship; tutoring toolbox)
   key points about setting up
      programmes 57–58
   outcomes 1–3
   questioning protocol 70
tutoring relationship 3–4, 44, 49, 60–61, 72
   see also expectations; obligations
      to tutors; reciprocity; sense of
      agreement
   building a strong relationship 9–19
   and development of metacognitive
      skills 70
   and goal setting 65–66, 72

key points 29
positioning within school, community and family 9, 29, 52–53, 55, 68–69
tutoring techniques 4–5, 45
see also elements of a tutoring session
tutoring toolbox 5, 36, 44, 73
applying to common student issues 42–43
facilitation ideas 43–44
key points 45
tools
ask a deep explanatory question 40–41, 42
assess prior knowledge 41, 42
contextualise a specific task within a bigger picture 39, 42
demonstrate a process or exercise 36–37, 43
describe a basic process 39–40
determine an initial course of action 38–39, 42
give specific descriptive feedback 41–42, 43
give the student a task to do 37, 42
identify a specific problem 38, 42
tutors
disclosure of relevant personal information 34
engagement with goal-setting 13, 64
grit test 28–29
growth mindset 25
payment 53–54
recruiting 47, 48–49, 53, 54
as role models 8
similarity in age and experience to students 3
training 47, 49, 51–52, 53, 58, 70, 71, 72, 73–74

visibility of thinking 31, 63, 70

www.ingramcontent.com/pod-product-compliance
Lightning Source LLC
Chambersburg PA
CBHW080637230426
43663CB00016B/2901